adultery &
other private matters

adultery & other private matters

your right to personal freedom in marriage

Lonny Myers, M.D.

Hunter Leggitt, M.Div.

Drawings by Jesse Martinez

Nelson-Hall Chicago

Library of Congress Cataloging in Publication Data
Myers, Lonny.
　　Adultery & other private matters.

　　Includes index.
　　1. Sex in marriage.　2. Intimacy (Psychology)
3. Privacy, Right of—United States.　I. Leggitt,
Hunter, joint author.　II. Title.
HQ734.M984　301.41'53　75-4701
ISBN 0-911012-51-6

Manufactured in the United States of America

This book is dedicated to all who have made sacrifices so that we might have the time and energy for its completion, and to our readers. May you find the space you need to live, to grow, to experience your own being and the being of others in richest measure.

. . . And to D.J.—H.L.

contents

INTRODUCTION

SELFHOOD IN MARRIAGE

We recognize that most modern concepts of marriage stress togetherness, requiring that all experiences be open and shared with one's spouse. However, our marriage model includes private free time for each spouse within the limits of responsibility. We call this private free time Compartment Four. It is not offered as a universal prescription, but as an option.

This book tells how marriage can be made more flexible, so that the need for truly independent activities need not break the marriage contract, create guilt feelings, or be destructive. Our purpose is not to berate those couples who throughout marriage choose to share everything. However, we believe that for many persons there can be a greater advantage to retaining a potential for unshared experiences, a part of oneself that remains unmarried.

Since people have different capacities for growth, different directions of growth, different degrees of imagination, and changing levels of expectations, complete sharing of frustrations and wishful fantasies will often cause anxiety and conflict. Many marriage partners withhold nega-

tive feelings out of kindness and consideration while presenting an outward image of complete sharing.

Even in unusually intimate marriages, one or both partners may begin to fantasize about, and later actively wish for, certain experiences that could not be shared comfortably. These yearnings often grow stronger and more insistent over the years, finally presenting a dilemma that once would have been unthinkable: personal growth and stimulation versus marital togetherness. Divorce is not the only way to resolve the dilemma. This book presents an alternative that makes room for autonomous activities without destroying the marriage.

Compartment Four can range from a few unshared fantasies to the stereotyped double life where a major portion of one's aspirations and experiences are outside of the marriage. It is not a new term for old-fashioned clandestine affairs, although extramarital affairs are by no means excluded. In fact, there is virtually no limit to the activities Compartment Four might include. But whatever is included, it is in no way to be regarded as cheating or taking something away from your spouse. On the contrary, it affirms the positive values of independent, autonomous decisions and activities by each partner in a marriage.

Kahlil Gibran expressed this idea in *The Prophet:*

But let there be spaces in your togetherness . . .
For the pillars of the temple stand apart,
And the oak tree and the cypress grow not in each other's shadow.

chapter 1

how to be lively
in a dull marriage

The restrictions of traditional marriage often cause undue frustration and push people towards divorce, when all they really wanted was a little more personal freedom. Many marriages that now end in divorce might have continued as viable marriages if the partners had recognized their need for personal freedom, and had accepted the basic concept proposed in this book: the right to independent, private activities for each partner.

The authors recognize the countless married persons who have found excitement or contentment within conventional marriage, who feel no particular need for unconventional lifestyles. We rejoice whenever personal fulfillment does not conflict with marital togetherness. We also recognize the countless others for whom marriage has become an unending source of tension and misery, for whom divorce is the best choice.

But most couples are somewhere between these two extremes. One or both partners feel more or less trapped by marriage, but still the trap offers many rewards. If you are typical of persons in this middle group, your marriage provides many satisfactions, but still you experience a yearning to enjoy independent friendships and activities that seem incompatible with marital togetherness. You may be asking, is it really necessary to sacrifice personal growth and freedom to make my marriage work?

Our intention is to offer strategies and concepts that will allow you to grow in your own direction, limited by practical considerations, but less limited by the rules, tastes or whims of your partner. In return, of course, you will recognize that a certain amount of independence and privacy may be just as desirable and beneficial for your partner as it is for you. By integrating the right to autonomy and privacy for each partner into your marriage contract, you can lessen the anxiety and guilt feelings that so often result when one partner engages in private activities that are not shared with the other. Thus, even the most unexciting marriage need not force the partners to become dull persons.

Yet the feeling of being trapped is a common complaint of married people. Although the responsibilities of marriage are quite real, especially when there are children to rear, we still believe that many spouses would benefit from more freedom to pursue purely personal interests. We have definite reservations about people who neglect their children while satisfying themselves. But on the other hand, on the basis of observation, we are convinced that many parents are better parents when they also have time to do their own thing.

Of course, the amount of time and what one does with it depends on family finances, number of children, and many other limiting factors. Our argument is that in principle, and as time and other factors allow, within the limits of responsible behavior, the option of personal pursuits that are not shared with spouse or children is a basic right of everyone.

Conventional marriage clearly does not work for everyone. It works when each partner grows gradually and in a way quite acceptable to the other and when there are no sudden changes that seem to threaten the marriage relationship. This is the model held up for all to follow, with the clear implication of failure if your growth pattern does not dovetail with your spouse's.

We believe that how spouses handle their differences is often more important to the success or failure of a marriage than how many common interests they share. But prior to marriage, during the courtship stage of a relationship, couples have a tendency to gloss over their differences. The reasons for this have been described in detail by G. R. Bach and R. M. Deutsch in their book entitled *Pairing*. The mutual deception of courting is not motivated by ill will, but by the desires of two individuals to see each other as good marriage bets. In our family-oriented society, people who are single are usually at a disadvantage. It is often harder for single people, especially women, to rent or buy an apartment, to obtain a good credit rating, and so forth. There are tax advantages to being married. Insurance rates are higher for most singles. And then, there is often the suspicion that if you are still single beyond a certain age, you are somehow immature, neurotic, undeveloped, or undesirable. This is especially true of women. Most of society's pressures push us in the direction of marriage, and singles form a distinct minority group. Therefore, in the words of Bach and Deutsch, "it is only natural to want to escape from minority status to respectability. And the pressure is added to by embarrassed families and concerned friends."

For these reasons, people play the dating game, which is really a search for a marriage partner. They tend to look for tastes and interests that they have in common with dates, and to ignore or suppress whatever doesn't conveniently fit. This is especially true when a person is considered a good marriage bet, and the other one wants to make an especially good impression. Basic differences in values, enthusiasms, and life goals are often overlooked in the rush towards the altar.

It is all well and good to say that this well-intentioned mutual deception during dating shouldn't occur. But it does. Therefore, interests and values that were never discussed during courting may surface as surprises years after the vows are sealed. In addition, if both partners continue to grow as persons after marriage, they often grow at different rates and in different directions. At the same time, activities that provided hours of mutual joy early in the marriage may now have lost all fascination for one or both partners. When one tries to reach out to a new activity, he or she may feel a strong pull backwards, as though the partner were holding one back in a three-legged race. But you may question, "I have two legs and you have two legs; must we run a three-legged race?" (For those unfamiliar with this game, a three-legged

race is run with one of your legs bound to one of your partner's legs.)

If the pull toward outside activities is strong, even though the marriage offers satisfactions, many persons consider divorce—often without considering how they might build more latitude for personal interests within the marriage.

To such persons, many conservative people might offer this advice: if you maintain an income and home, and do not abuse each other physically, you can always find sufficient conventional pastimes for a wholesome and good life. Such well-meaning advice frequently comes from persons in the counseling profession, many of whom live lives of quiet desperation themselves and cannot comprehend any great urgency for excitement or grand feelings of joy and aliveness. These conservative attitudes might be summarized as: there is no need to reach out— appreciate what you have.

However, we see no contradiction between appreciating what you have, yet reaching out to find additional fulfillment. For example, there are many marriages in which the sex is great, but there is little real companionship such as good conversation, playing and laughing to-gether, enjoying mutual nonsexual interests. Clearly, partners in such marriages might indeed yearn for an evening spent with someone who truly enjoys gourmet food and stimulating conversation. We see no reason why such companionship dates should threaten a marriage. The concept of dating after marriage appears later in this book.

To deal with a more complex situation, we also see no need to arbitrarily exclude sex from the categories of experience that some persons might want or need outside of their marriages. Although it is clear and amply documented that extramarital sex is a factor in the break-up of many marriages, we will present the other side of the story to demonstrate how some persons enjoy extramarital sexual affairs without hurting their marriages.

Our quarrel with some of the basic assumptions of the Puritan ethic and traditional marriage is that such traditions are arbitrarily limiting. Moreover, they are based on concepts of love and human relationships that were developed when it was impossible to separate sex from the risk of pregnancy. We are glad that some people seem to thrive within conventional marriage limits, but at the same time, we are concerned about the many people who seem unable to do so, no matter how hard they try. Many such persons have worked at marriage, they have visited the counselors and sex clinics and have attempted to develop "wholesome" mutual interests, but they continue to yearn for something that their marriages are unable to provide. We believe that a wider latitude in marriage to pursue different and individual pursuits is often preferable to divorce. Often the problem lies in the limiting nature of the traditional marriage contract, rather than in any insurmountable flaw in the relationship between the two people. This problem cannot be solved by leaving one conventional marriage for another with a different partner. The problem remains. We would like to expand the limits and allow more room for personal decisions, in contrast to decisions made by the couple together.

But first, here is our list of seven basic assumptions that are at the heart of the Puritan ethic and the traditional marriage ideal:

1. The more you have to give up for something, the more it must be worth.
2. To make personal decisions and to have relationships that are not acceptable to the spouse is selfish and unnecessary.
3. Excitement and stimulation are luxuries to be enjoyed only if they occur within the conventional boundaries of marriage. They are not worth taking risks for and should not be actively sought outside marriage.

4. The answer to most marriage problems is to work harder at making the marriage work.
5. Love is a magical state which, when combined with marriage, can fulfill all one's intimate needs.
6. Honesty is the best policy, especially in marriage.
7. If the marriage is not working out despite all of the above, think twice about the hardships of divorce and the social stigma. But if life is still unbearable, get a divorce.

Rene Dubos was not writing about marriage, but about attitudes towards life in general, when he said in his book *The God Within:* "He [man] knows that he can find biological happiness by achieving adaptation to his physical and social environment, but he realizes that this form of happiness is as limited in scope as the contentment of a cow." It is clear that for many married persons, the marriage is the principal element in their social environment. Not only is marriage assumed by society to be the major permissible source of closeness between two people, but it also helps to determine how one fits into the community, both socially and economically. One's marriage style, including such presumably personal choices as whether or not a wife takes on a full-time job, is an important area in which one is often asked to make sacrifices in order to adapt. As Dubos points out, it is possible to achieve a certain degree of happiness by simply adapting, but this may be as limited as the contentment of a cow. We point this out because the third assumption regarding traditional marriage listed above stated that excitement and stimulation are acceptable luxuries but only if they just happen; they are not worth risking the status quo. In contrast, Dubos seems to imply that simply adapting is a far cry from fulfilling one's human potential.

The concept that human life should move beyond adaptation to include such items as peak experiences was also stressed by psychologist A. H. Maslow, in *Towards a Psychology of Being.* Of course, a number of persons experience such peaks within outwardly conventional marriages. But there are many others whose marital experience lacks peaks, and it is there that the question of adaptation versus risk arises.

It is for these persons—who want to be married and yet remain free

to make independent decisions and to seek additional relationships—
that we offer this alternative set of assumptions:

1. What a relationship is worth depends on what it contributes
   to one's personal fulfillment and the spread of warmth and
   aliveness among others. If such a relationship is easy to come
   by, it may be valuable nonetheless. A relationship (e.g., marriage) can be valuable for what latitude it allows as well as the
   satisfaction it provides.

2. Spouses need not demand of each other that all purely personal
   decisions and relationships be mutually acceptable. One
   should be able to respond to such interests to the maximum,
   within responsible limits.

3. Excitement, stimulation, and feeling "turned on" are important in varying degrees to different persons. For some people,
   marriage provides peak experiences and they feel little need to
   seek additional stimulation outside of marriage. But for many
   others, independent activities can be important sources of
   excitement and joy. If such emotions are important to a married person who does not experience them within marriage, it
   should not be necessary to "burn all bridges" in order to seek
   them.

4. The answer to many marriage problems is to stay alive and
   warm as an individual, whether the sources of aliveness and
   warmth be found inside or outside the marriage. When
   fulfilled as a person, an individual is more likely to be capable
   of positive responses to others and to responsibilities at home.

5. A limited sense of fulfillment is to be derived from one's
   marriage partner. Love, in or out of marriage, is many things,
   but one thing it is not is a magic process that attends to all of
   one's needs for an indefinite length of time.

6. Honesty is not always the best policy. We do not urge total
   honesty between spouses as advocated in the book, *Open Marriage.* We can see many situations in which honesty would be
   much too threatening to the spouse and might well jeopardize
   the marital relationship. The assumption that honesty is not
   always the best policy allows for the development of the un-

foreseen, for the possibility of discreet experiences that are fulfilling for one partner at a time when the other partner is either unable or unwilling to accept this independent decision.

7. When marriage lacks excitement, emotional closeness, peak experiences—but remains benign, neither disrespectful nor violent—divorce is not the only way to gain freedom for personal growth. An option is to be less tightly dependent, placing fewer expectations on the marriage and allowing more room for independent decisions.

These assumptions are realistic bases for combining the security of marriage with the possibility of further exploration and growth. To quote Rene Dubos, "Modern man still craves both adventure and the comfort of the familiar; in fact he probably needs both for his mental health."

Such assumptions are appropriate for persons who are relatively affluent and who live in large metropolitan areas, where three out of four Americans now live. Affluent city dwellers enjoy an unprecedented amount of free time, mobility, and anonymity. Our point is not merely that sexual opportunities are more numerous, and discretion is more likely to succeed, but that the potential of extramarital sexual relations is clearly an important element of feeling free for many persons. We are equally in favor of opening other doors that could lead to nonsexual opportunities available in today's urban setting. We stress this because in many marriages there still seems to be resistance to any meaningful outside activities other than work, that the couple does not do together or report in detail. Strangely enough, even the swingers—couples who meet with other couples for sexual exchanges or group sex—offer this motto: the couple that swings together stays together! Our concern in this book has more to do with the freedom for individual marriage partners to make independent decisions in a context of personal free time than it has to do with sex per se. Clearly, swinging offers great latitude for sexual encounters when both spouses are present, but almost no latitude for independent individual fulfillment.

The shift toward more opportunity for individual experiences is most dramatic for urban, sophisticated women, but we believe there is enough general truth in our seven points to have meaning for both sexes, everywhere in America. One couple we interviewed came from a community of 500 but boasted of the personal independence each spouse had to seek outside fulfillment. They felt that this latitude had enhanced their marriage over a period of many, many years.

Many facets of one's self are typically not shared before marriage. Predictably, these are personal interests, values, and even talents that never seem to fit the ideal marriage. When these hidden dimensions come out later to enrich the marital relationship, that is indeed desirable. It is less so when they are revealed only to become a source of conflict. For example, many women once pretended to be somewhat stupid and helpless in order to flatter the male ego. Some persons were able to practice these protective deceptions for a lifetime, ostensibly, and perhaps realistically, for the sake of the marriage. Some of those deceptions could have been serious because personal values, strong feelings, or potential growth were repressed. Whatever personal qualities, values, feelings, or growth potentials that cannot be expressed in the context of a particular marriage are lost unless the marriage also provides ample free time for each partner. In the absence of opportunities for expression, important aspects of one's self are lost, which becomes abundantly clear as one grows older and looks back on what might have been.

To carry the logic of the togetherness motif to its illogical conclusion, we now present a wholly fictitious story about a couple who did everything together even if that meant doing nothing. The unlikely couple are named Rita and Herb.

In the early days of their marriage, it was so exciting for Rita and Herb to spend time together that their individual needs were consumed in the compelling warmth of romantic love. Their primary source of joy was *with whom* they did various things rather than *what* they did. That is, it was more important for each to be with the other than to engage in his own favorite activities.

Although Herb was an atheist, he went to church with Rita because he wanted to be with her more than he wanted to avoid church. True to the dating game, characterized by well-meaning mutual deception, Herb never mentioned his actual religious beliefs.

Rita accompanied Herb on Saturday nights to the club where his jazz band played. It was such fun to see him perform and for her to know that he knew she was there. Rita never mentioned to him that she really didn't like jazz and strongly preferred classical music.

Now it is several years later. Rita and Herb have each made sacrifices to make their marriage work. Now that romantic love has faded, they find themselves in a double bind. They continue to believe that married couples ought to do almost everything together, and this belief is reinforced by articles they read in the popular press and ideas they see reflected in movies and television.

They have escaped from this bind by tacitly agreeing that each will abstain from those activities that they can no longer comfortably do together. Now that the illusions of romantic love have faded, Herb can't tolerate sitting through a church service. So Rita doesn't go either.

Religious and ethical tenets recognize that sins of omission are just as important as sins of commission. However, Rita and Herb share the all too popular belief that one can be good simply by not doing anything bad. This is a negative, sterile goodness. Another ethical distinction can be made between living life according to one's own conscience and reason, and merely following the herd. Conformity to a marriage partner can be as ethically shallow as any other kind of conformity. Marital conformity can consist of pleasing one's partner while engaging in activities that conflict with one's own standards and preferences. It can also include sitting on one's hands to avoid activities that one's partner disapproves. Rita and Herb conformed to each other in the negative sense. Rather than having led each other down paths of folly, which might at least have been more fun, they have simply inhibited each other's personal desires.

Some of the results are:

1.   Rita wanted to go back to school. Herb, however, only finished high school and is implicitly fearful that Rita will outgrow him. Some marriage counselors might advise them to go to school together. As a matter of fact, Rita and Herb considered that, but Herb failed the entrance examinations. So Rita buried her intellectual stirrings to conform to the marriage.

2.   Herb used to love well-seasoned foods. Rita dislikes foreign

fare. Some counselors might suggest that she learn to cook in the style he prefers. At first, she tried, and he tried to pretend to enjoy the unfortunate results. Rita is no cook. Her attempts at *haute cuisine* were disasters. Herb will not allow himself to go to foreign restaurants without her, and she won't go. Gradually, his taste buds grow dull to tolerate her cooking.

3. Rita used to enjoy seeing Anne. They had been best friends since childhood. But Herb always acted freaky and strange when Anne came over for the evening. Though he didn't come right out and say it, Rita got the message. She no longer sees Anne, and is gradually letting all her outside friendships grow cold to comply with what she feels are the requirements of marital togetherness.

4. Herb used to enjoy golf. Rita, now resentful about giving up her friendship with Anne, refers to "silly men chasing a little white ball around a pasture when there are lawns to be raked and eaves to be cleaned at home." Herb has almost given up golf. He feels so much conflict whenever he plays that it spoils his fun. He doesn't get to the eaves, either, and has grown flabby to fit the marriage.

5. Rita used to think that her volunteer work at the school for the deaf expressed a vital side of her, but Herb kept calling her a do-gooder and, perhaps because he was resentful about giving up golf, said that charity should begin at home.

6. Not surprisingly, their sex life is also growing dull. What Rita enjoys most, Herb dislikes, and vice versa. Early in their relationship, the glow of romance made it easier to pretend and they shared the illusion of a perfect sexual pairing. But now, true to the negative style of their togetherness, they'd rather watch television in order to avoid exposing their inner feelings of dissatisfaction with their sex life. After the late show, both are just too tired. They are good by virtue of not doing anything bad, even if that means being good for nothing.

It might be said of this imaginary couple that only a couple of jellyfish would allow this degree of attrition to take place. Yet such reversals of the growth process in the name of togetherness are familiar to all of us, even if seldom so extreme. The result is that marriage partners often become smaller, more confined, less interesting persons.

Rita gave up church for Herb, and Herb gave up golf for Rita, and Rita gave up Anne for Herb, and Herb gave up, and so it has gone until now. If this pattern continues, the day will come when each will have given up everything for nothing! For each will be a nothing. The marriage itself will become nothing, with nobody married to nobody.

In the case of Rita and Herb, there **were too** many intrinsic conflicts glossed over during courtship for them to ever have had the kind of positive togetherness that a few compatible couples can enjoy.

It is easy to say that this couple might just as well face the facts and get a divorce. Indeed, divorce has become alarmingly common in recent years even among couples who are much more compatible than Rita and Herb.

But let us suppose that Rita and Herb now have several children, a mortgage on a lovely home, and, although they are considered dull, they are also esteemed as the kind of solid couple that makes them good credit risks, and good neighbors, and makes Herb the kind of family man that his company likes to promote. Although divorce would not be the end of the world for them, the disadvantages are obvious.

We believe that a Compartment Four, private time for each spouse to engage in independent activities, can make marriage more viable for many such persons. It provides time for activities and relationships that are very important to one partner, but would either bore the other partner or create marital conflict if the other partner were involved.

We recognize that many readers will agree up to but definitely excluding outside sex. Many will say that extramarital sex is irresponsible by itself, regardless of the positive or negative consequences, or because the odds are against any positive outcome, so much so that the risk itself is irresponsible.

We do not believe that outside sex is either easy to handle or risk free. However, we do believe that if extramarital sex is going to occur, then it is much more likely to produce a positive outcome when each spouse has some private time completely on his or her own, with no strings attached, and when each partner respects the other's privacy as an inviolable sanctuary.

Marshall Bryant Hodge, a psychologist, comments on such affairs in *Your Fear of Love*. In his view, "if the basic relationship with the spouse is not too hopelessly unsatisfying and if the principals do not react precipitously, a marriage often survives extramarital affairs. In fact, it may be strengthened as a result of a new-found ability to be open to the experience and expression of love. But society's attitude about extramarital affairs often operates against the survival of a marriage."

We know individuals who have private time and never use it for sexual liaisons. For some, it would violate their personal standards of behavior. Private free time is not a vacation from one's own conscience. Others feel that they could not handle outside sex even though they desire it. Finally there are those whose unmet needs are neither sexual nor romantic.

From time to time throughout this book, the reader will encounter somewhat whimsical parables and fantasy images set apart from the main text. For the authors, these represented a change of pace from expository prose. Although to us these images are important, they may not be to you. We felt no need to be grimly serious throughout.

In our culture, marriage is the biggest package under the Christmas tree, in whatever shape you dream of, wrapped in gold, and with all the

corroborating rattles that say, when you shake it, "It is that! It is! It is the sled!"

But then comes Christmas. In a package shaped just like the big red sled in Macy's window with ribbons and papers flying, comes a croquet set with three missing wickets.

How could anyone have mistaken the rattle of a croquet set for a big red sled? Our hopes deceive us, after all. What if you don't like croquet? Or maybe you like it, but it's winter, and you're the only kid on the block without a sled?

We must also consider the feelings of the croquet set!

Don't we often make ourselves appear to be different than we are in order to be wanted, to be the big, shiny, most beautiful package under the tree? "I think he wants a big red sled. I'll look like one till Christmas!"

But Christmas morning always comes and there you are—a poor little croquet set with three missing wickets.

If only there could be a sled for winter, and a croquet set for spring, and a beach ball for summer, and a rake for fall bonfires. One could love each of them but at different times.

"Shall I, a croquet set, try to be a beach ball, and a sled, and a rake according to the season? Or, being myself, shall my lover be happy only when the grass is green but unhappy when the beach is warm, the autumn leaves descend, or the snow drifts on the hill?

"But no, I may not share my house with a rake, a beach ball, and a sled. Nor may my lover borrow one of those, even for a day. And even if I didn't really mind, it's considered untoward and wicked on our block to borrow other folks' gifts. That being so, too much is expected of me and I really would like to change the rules. They say that the only way to get another intimacy present is to give the old one back. I don't want to be given back! Couldn't we change the rules so I could just be me?"

Many of us who are caught in this dilemma will not sacrifice either ourselves or our marriages. For our marriages offer many satisfactions. And yet, we have additional needs, and there is much yearning. We are moved or attracted tenderly toward people and activities outside our marriages. We do not blame our spouses for this, for who can be all things to all people? Yet outside interests are usually viewed as particularly threatening when they are enjoyed with attractive persons of the other sex. If you enjoy golf but your partner doesn't, you are allowed to play golf but often only with friends of the same sex. But if you love ballroom dancing and your partner loathes it, the rubrics of conventional marriage would forbid your dancing. So dancing is eliminated as a recreation for many, not because dancing is bad, but because of our strict limitations of partners. Too often and too much pleasure passes us by for the sake of togetherness.

In that regard we would like to quote four stanzas from Ibsen's *Peer Gynt*. Although Ibsen was not commenting on marriage, but on the pursuit of wealth and pleasure, the important point was that Peer had sacrificed much of his better self in their pursuit. Need we add that many persons do the same in the name of marriage? Nowhere else have we found such eloquent shorthand for the regrets of those who have propitiated the gods of conventional marriage by the sacrifice of their better selves.

Threadballs

We are thoughts;
You should have thought us;
Little feet, to life
You should have brought us!
We should have risen
With glorious sound;
But here like threadballs
We are earthbound. . . .

A Sighing in the Air

We are songs;
You should have sung us!
In the depths of your heart
Despair has wrung us!
We lay and waited;
You called us not.
May your throat and voice
With poison rot.

Dewdrops

We are tears
Which were never shed.
The cutting ice
Which all hearts dread
We could have melted;
But now its dark
Is frozen into
A stubborn heart.
The wound is closed;
Our power is lost.

Broken Straws

We are deeds
You have left undone;
Strangled by doubt,
Spoiled ere begun.
At the Judgment Day
We shall be there
To tell our tale.
How will you fare?

chapter 2

Oating after marriage

Compartment Four marriage makes dating after marriage—that is, dating someone other than your spouse—an intriguing possibility.

For dating is fun! Of course not all dates turn out to be fun. But a date explicitly sets up an opportunity not otherwise provided—an opportunity for a one-to-one relationship, unchaperoned. To face another human being in that way—exchanging glances and expressions and quiet words without regard to a third party—can be one of life's most rewarding experiences.

Nevertheless, most of us think of the dating age as a transitional period lasting from adolescence to marriage. Dating is seen primarily as a search for a partner, part of the pairing-off process that leads inevitably to marriage and the rearing of a family. Dating is not seriously considered by most people as a uniquely rewarding and on-going way to relate to other people.

Instead, once we pair off—in marriage, going steady, or in a live-in arrangement—there are always limitations to the acceptable ways of relating to third parties: limited touch, limited eye contact, limited isolation, limited intimacy.

Why? Society treats sex as though it were a time bomb between our legs and such intimacy would set it off. Otherwise responsible adults would be swept away by uncontrollable orgies with their marriages shattered, children weeping and tragedy spreading in all directions.

With regard to the dire consequences of extramarital sex, these can well happen! We don't dispute it. What we do dispute is the notion that sex by itself is the culprit. Is it the "emotional involvement" then? We don't think so.

The danger of outside sex derives from its context. If the context is an exclusive-possessive lifestyle, then extramarital sex seems to prevent having both a lover and a marriage partner. If the lover is also an exclusivist, he or she will be trying to beat out the marriage partner and win the prize. At the same time, there is the inevitable comparison between one's lover and one's partner in the sense of which one is "best." This is indeed a competitive and potentially destructive situation, and it's very difficult for anyone to come up smelling like a rose.

But for nonpossessive people, the context is quite different. For them, love does not have to be exclusive to be real and valuable. There is much less of an either–or consequence implied by attractions to third parties, or dating, loving, becoming emotionally involved, and sometimes enjoying sex with them.

If your marriage, or other form of partnership, is liberated, you may be far more emotionally involved with your partner than with anyone else. And you may enjoy sex with your partner more than with others. You may love him or her the most. However, you don't tend to think in those terms; the "more," "most," and "best" aren't terribly important. People can be different from each other without necessarily being better or worse. This makes it possible to enjoy a wider range of people and experiences, and to do so more fully.

This is not to say that nonpossessive people don't have priorities. When there are pressing needs at home, the family must of course come first. We are normally more committed to some people than to others. And marriage is that kind of commitment. So is the decision to rear children. So is a job, for that matter. When we don't know what our priorities are, we tend to be confused and in trouble.

But there is a tremendous difference between having priorities and being exclusive. The difference is experienced when priorities do not really conflict. For example, when Susan—whose marriage is liberated—is asked out for a drink after work, she decides not to go because of her commitment to be home when the children arrive from school. But she might suggest having lunch together tomorrow, when there are no conflicting priorities. For Jane, however, this situation is not seen as a matter of priorities. She feels it is wrong to have drinks alone with other men—and the more attracted she feels toward a particular man, the more so! She is not inwardly free to enjoy a potentially exciting person even when there is no priority conflict. She regards dating other men as an *a priori* evil, an act of disloyalty in and of itself, whether or not the date would actually affect her partner's love.

Of course, exclusive-possessive people often have affairs because they have as many unfulfilled needs as anyone else. But in terms of the insights of transactional analysis, such affairs may become battlegrounds between one's parent messages saying no and one's rebellious inner child saying, "to hell with you!" The affair then becomes potentially destructive.

In addition, the love affairs of exclusive-possessive people tend to have hidden agendas. You will remember the games and counter moves in the play, *Who's Afraid of Virginia Wolff?* One of the games was "get the guests!" The hidden agenda of an affair is sometimes "get the spouse!" If so, the spouse is actually the main actor. "Wouldn't he croak if he could see me now?" one fantasizes. It is the spouse, who may never appear on stage, whose presence in the wings determines all the action. Thus the lover is not really the star, but a pawn in a marital game.

But this is hardly possible if the spouse is not an exclusive-possessive person! Of course it's true that some people pose as nonjealous types as part of a counter game. "Hit me!" begs the masochist. "No!" replies the sadist, disdainfully.

Such convoluted behavior tends to be largely absent from the extramarital behavior of nonpossessive people. The excitement tends to be in the affair itself. The lover is truly loved rather than being used as a mere pawn. Clandestine behavior is not so much a turn-on as a necessity. One recognizes that the appearance of sexual monogamy remains important for getting most jobs, for social status, and perhaps, in the view of many, for one's children. And if one intuitively knows that one's spouse would be deeply hurt were he or she to know, every possible precaution should be taken to guard the privacy of the affair.

Currently, most extramarital relationships seem to be clandestine. Once you are forced to arrive separately, go into a room, and lock the door—what are the real options except for making love sexually?

But dating after marriage allows you to go on a picnic or an all-day skiing trip, walk along the beach, go to the zoo, a symphony, or to an art museum. Dating after marriage allows all the romantic touches such as gazing into each other's eyes over candlelight and wine, or attending the theater together.

That is why the anti-daters will be quite mistaken if they view dating after marriage as an open encouragement for outside sex. For in fact, dating gives more options to people who want to be intimate without explicit sex. There are many persons who would enjoy intimacy without any interaction of the genitalia, who now must meet either behind closed doors or not at all.

Anti-daters may also use the weak argument that dating after marriage would be an escape. If so, we say, "Right on!" A wholesome, healthy, rewarding escape! How marvelous it can be to relate to someone without taking them into your orbit of everyday chores and problems. You don't have to live with their faults, or they with yours. Instead, you can put problems aside for a while and just have fun.

Another kind of dating after marriage is for comfort—a sympathetic ear to hear your complaints, a shoulder to cry on if the need arises. Anti-daters might insist that this should be the role of one's spouse or live-in partner. But that isn't necessarily so! If one's partner has just lost a job and is depressed and upset, additional woes are not needed. Most of us would try to make life more pleasant and reassuring, keeping our own sadness and frustration to ourselves for the time being. To do otherwise often makes things worse. But we need someone to listen to us, too! Instead of always being with a neighbor or a friend of the same sex, a date might make certain revelations more meaningful. When the distress is over, the mutual closeness of having comforted and been comforted can often bring a warmth, a glow, and even a joy that seldom follows griping to a neighbor. Dating after marriage definitely includes such comforting dates.

In addition to escape dates and comforting dates, a third kind of dating after marriage is the Good Samaritan date. There is nothing patronizing in our use of the words "Good Samaritan." The primary motive cannot be pity because that would spoil it. But although each party in a dating arrangement gets something out of it, there are certain inequalities in Good Samaritan dating. A date for someone who hasn't had one in six months will be like a mountain of anticipation and excitement rising above the flat plains of dull routine. But for the "Good Samaritan" who provides the excitement, the date may be only one of many fun evenings in a full life. In that sense, the "Good Samaritan" perceives that a small effort, with little or no realistic threat to other relationships, can bring a tremendous amount of joy and fulfillment into the life of another. That is rewarding enough by itself.

In that regard, many single or divorced or widowed women would definitely say, "Yes, I want to borrow a married man for a night of fun! I need a Good Samaritan!" The dangers are falling in love and wanting him to divorce his wife. Oh, yes, we are used to that stereotype. And it can happen. However, there are an increasing number of single women who would love to date but who definitely do not want to get married—and they mean it! Then, one might ask, why don't they just date single men who feel the same way? That remark is not only superficial but unrealistic. There are two reasons why dating other single people is easier said than done. The first is that while single men can often date women many years younger, it is more difficult for single women in their forties or fifties to date younger men. And even without this complicating factor, it cannot be denied that there are many more available women over forty-five than men in that age group. The number of women between the ages of thirty and forty-five who would like dates but don't have them is nearly as great. If such a woman, wanting a fun date but not a marriage partner, dates a married man, clearly this can provide both of them with a warm and rewarding evening without necessarily threatening the man's marriage.

In that regard, one single woman in her forties says, "I've got three guys I've been seeing off and on for about eight years. Bob is married and comes in from New York three or four times a year. He's lots of fun to go out with. He doesn't know many people here, so we go wherever we want—good restaurants, shows, the symphony, museums, anywhere.

"I'm also seeing Harry once a week or so. If I had to marry the guy, he'd drive me batty in about ten days. No way! So do I threaten his wife? You've got to be kidding. He's a damned good lover, though. Good thing, too, because what else is there to do when you're hiding in a motel room? He doesn't dare to come to my place more than two or three times a year. Somebody seeing his car there just once and telling his wife is too great a risk, he thinks.

"But the strangest one is Jim. His wife is my best friend. And she knows all about us! About the sex? There isn't any! Never! I think it would be good, and I kind of want it. But things would get too complicated. So what do we do? Skiing, skin-diving, movies, any old thing. Sex? Never. You think my pal Sally is home brooding while we're out? Jealous? Biting her nails? Hell, no. She's a writer, and Jim really bugs her when she's working. So sometimes she'll call me up and say, 'Hey Sue, will you get this guy out of my hair tonight?'"

Rarely in life is everything so smooth and open for all concerned. The fact that Sue does not want to get married reduces the potential for conflict.

Still, there are single women who would very much like to get married someday. Dating after marriage can also work between married men and such single women, but only when it is clearly understood that he is not the potential marriage partner and the date is to be strictly a fun time for both. That distinction may not always be easy to make and maintain. Yet, for a woman with no marriage-potential dates in sight, when the realistic probability is another six months with no evenings out, why not have a playful date with a married man? In this context, one man could date more than one girl and vice versa. In such instances, if a real date with a marriage potential comes up for the woman, her already-married occasional date must be ready to step aside. The most important point here is the absolute necessity to be open and clear at all times about what the relationship means and—just as important—

what it does not mean. If this can be accomplished, it can be beautiful. We see this as very iffy.

In the above examples, there are many risks. There may be mistakes. But we see no reason to exclude the possibility. It is necessary to weigh the pros and cons on a case by case basis and then make an informed decision.

Dating after marriage might also work rather well for a married woman and a confirmed bachelor who finds most single girls so hell bent on marriage that he can't relax and enjoy them. But with a married woman who has no intention of leaving her husband, he feels quite at ease and loves to lavish attention on her and squire her about town. Neither one's marriage (or singleness!) is threatened, and both of them have a good time.

We also suggest a fourth kind of dating after marriage for your consideration. And we have no name for it. Perhaps "added-dimension dating" would do, if it could add another dimension to a friendship between two couples.

Consider the case of Alan and Sarah, whose best friends are Mike and Lorna. They are typical of today's couple friendships. Sometimes Alan-and-Sarah go over to Mike-and-Lorna's. Sometimes the two couples go out together. And sometimes, the boys go shopping while the girls drink beer and watch the football game on TV.

However, Alan and Lorna don't do things alone—just the two of them. And neither do Mike and Sarah. In our view, this leaves a void—a missing dimension. As things stand, we have these relationships:

Alan and Sarah—Mike and Lorna
Sarah—Lorna
Alan—Mike
(Alan—Lorna)
(Mike—Sarah)

The parentheses indicate that the last two of these possible relationships are there but definitely limited. Alan and Lorna are not able to discover each other in a one-to-one relationship. Neither are Mike and Sarah. In a sense, they are friends-in-law, which is quite different from being true friends. Even when they are together as couples, there is definitely limited touching, eye contact, and intimacy between them.

Anything of that sort might evoke a "Hey, what's going on, anyway?" response from the respective spouses.

However, if Alan's basic commitment is to Sarah, and hers to Alan; and Mike's basic commitment is to Lorna, and hers to him, we feel that the friendship between the two couples might be enriched if Alan has the opportunity to become Lorna's friend on a one-to-one basis, while Mike and Sarah enjoy the same.

Again, this raises the spectre of sexuality, spouse swapping, and all the other bugaboos. Added-dimension dating across the lines of couple-friendships might be very difficult for exclusive-possessive people. But again, we are talking about dating which, unlike the clandestine sexual affairs to which we have become accustomed, opens up all kinds of possibilities for other things to do. Suppose, for example, that Alan and Lorna love art, while Mike and Sarah are definitely turned off by the idea of an afternoon at an art museum. The answer seems rather obvious—but our exclusive-possessive hang-ups prevent many people from arriving at a solution. We think it is clear that added-dimension dating for nonpossessive people would greatly enrich the lives of many without any undue risk to their respective marriages. It could add the missing dimension in couple-couple friendships.

In all of these examples of dating after marriage—escape dates, comforting dates, Good Samaritan dates, and added-dimension dates—we do not mean to dismiss or treat the potential risks lightly. But we want to point out and also take into account the fact that life and risks are synonymous. Nothing ventured, nothing gained. A family vacation trip is surely rewarding, but we know that every time we drive a car we take our lives into our hands or, more properly, take it out of our hands and put it in the hands of others. Then shall we give up vacations with the family? Despite Ralph Nader's revelations that many of us have been driving around in time bombs—with motors that slip and cut brake cables, heaters that give off poisonous fumes, accelerators that jam at turnpike speeds—how many of us have stopped driving cars?

Each time one takes a drink, there is the implied danger that one drink will lead to another and another and that if real stress overtakes one, what began as a nip may grow into alcoholism.

A few innocent ventures on the stock market, blessed as it is with all the virtues of Free Enterprise, sometimes turn into compulsive gambling.

When we ski, we risk breaking bones. There are many other examples, of course. And they all involve a certain amount of risk.

But without a willingness to run calculated risks, we would end up sitting in corners not even daring to light the logs in the fireplace for fear of burning the house down.

Therefore, when dating after marriage is realistically compared with currently practiced alternatives like clandestine affairs, cold or destructive marriages with no escape, or variety via divorce and remarriage, dating after marriage comes out as a strong contestant, in our view.

Consider what dating after marriage could mean in the lives of Ralph and Joan. They have been married for eleven years with two children, aged nine and seven.

Ralph's refrigeration business has been doing poorly recently. New, aggressive competition from a chain-store operation is pushing him out. While he is still able to provide reasonably well for his family, he is not able to be as flamboyantly generous as he once was. It hurts him to insist that they cut back on luxuries, yet he is forced to do so.

And his family has been cooperative. But whether or not there is really resentment on their part, he feels that there is—a silent resentment, an unspoken judgment that he is a failure. He either sees or reads into Joan's expression disappointment in him, a growing lack of respect. Without the success of earlier years, his self-respect suffers. And when Joan tries to reassure him by saying that business is bad for everyone, he feels neither comforted nor reassured. Just the opposite, he feels that she is patronizing him while secretly harboring doubts about his adequacy—that he is no longer a full-fledged man. And this has led to a degree of sexual impotence on his part. Here, too, he feels that Joan's forgiveness and patience are patronizing. And all of this brings home to him keenly and unbearably the fact that he isn't the man he used to be. As he gets on into middle age, time could make the situation worse.

Ralph doesn't want Joan's pity or sympathy. He doesn't want to confront her across the dinner table every night and read his failure in her eyes, as "Well, he isn't much, but he's mine."

Ralph knows Joan feels a commitment to him, for better or worse—that she is a loyal person who will take the bad with the good. He feels the same commitment to her. He would stick by her in times of stress. But this loyalty and commitment doesn't make him feel much better.

Lately, Ralph has slipped into self-protective, compulsive kinds of behavior. He reads the *New York Times* from first page to last. He sleeps more than he needs to on weekends. But during the week, he works at crossword puzzles late into the evening, avoiding the inevitable moment when he must get into bed with Joan. In effect, he is shutting her out as much as possible. He also finds himself turning away from the children more and more. He is too absorbed with his problems and too worried to be able to be sympathetic to their needs and problems.

Meanwhile, there is an attractive new secretary in Ralph's office. In recent weeks, he has felt himself drawn more and more to her. He is the boss and she respects him. Since she didn't know him in better days, she can't make unfavorable comparisons. He feels that she really approves of him, that she regards him as a man who has made a success of his life. This gives him a new sense of self, importance, and assurance.

And he would like to take her out, not necessarily to have a genital affair, but as a psychological haven. He feels that with her, he could simply relax and be himself, because she knows he is a success!

But can he take her out openly to plays, movies, for walks, or picnics? No, not unless he's willing to risk his standing in the community, which requires at least the appearance of sexual monogamy. Though he is just forty-three, he imagines that people are talking behind his back saying, "There's no fool like an old fool." So to see her, he must go to her apartment. And that would probably lead to sexual involvement which is not his primary need at this time. The third choice is to sink further into apathy, an apathy which could become a life-long habit.

What is happening to Joan in the meantime? She is suffering from Ralph's agonies. In addition, she is aware that the more she tries to reassure him, the more he resents her. She knows her reassurances only inflame his sense of failure. So she has given up. And she feels shut out and rejected. She looks into the mirror and says to herself, "I'm just thirty-eight and I'm already getting old and unattractive!" Joan also needs validation of herself. She needs the reassurance that she is still a desirable woman. But for the time being, Ralph is unable to give it to her.

If only Ralph and Joan can weather this storm, they may be all right. But how will they weather it?

Joan has thrown herself into community and hospital work, but these are not satisfying enough. She wants her old relationship with Ralph or, failing that, she wants some man to make her feel she's interesting and desirable. At parties, and even walking down the street, she finds herself eyeing men she passes as potential companions. But suppose she gets involved with someone? The town where she lives is very uptight about such things. She couldn't go out to dinner with him, or to a movie, or walk with him in the park. Again, what choices are presented by society?

Joan feels that she can't go on much longer in the existing circumstances. She's afraid that unless she finds some temporary relief, out of sheer frustration and fatigue, out of mounting anger and resentment, she may blow up and walk out or drive Ralph to walk out, and live to regret it.

So where can Joan turn? What can she do? What choices do our present mores offer her?

The answer, see a psychiatrist, is all too easy and glib. For her woes are real ones. Her need for warmth, for stroking, for a reassuring touch is a real, existential need. Her feelings of being rejected by Ralph reflect an accurate evaluation of what is really going on. And her assessment of the risks and dangers of an affair, even a nonsexual affair, is also realistic.

Given these facts, a psychiatrist or counselor might provide a sympathetic ear and a shoulder to cry on. But why should she pay $25 or $50 an hour for that? Even if she has deep problems (for example, relying too much on others for her own self-esteem), bills from a psychiatrist would add to Ralph's financial burden, hence his despair, and make the overall situation worse.

Why not a friend of the same sex, then? Joan has friends like that and she shares her troubles with them. But what she needs right now most of all is male-female affirmation, a man to whom she can be close, who will not push her away.

Joan and Ralph are among the many for whom dating after marriage is made to order. Dating after marriage does not explicitly exclude sex. But unlike most clandestine affairs, the context of dating does not put you on a situational escalator that almost inevitably leads to sex. Dating opens a whole new range of things to do together. Right now, Joan needs a Good Samaritan to take her out and away from her troubles —to provide an escape, to show her a good time, and to restore her confidence in herself as a woman. We are aware that many in the women's liberation movement will object to this implication that Joan's confidence in herself can only come from a man. We tend to agree with the objection—but we will let Joan be Joan for the time being, cultural conditioning being what it is. She does not need someone who wants to marry her, for she is truly committed to Ralph. She needs someone to love her now, someone who can gracefully let her go later on when things are better at home.

But with this society's mores, her choices appear to be to have a clandestine affair or to try to bluff things through with the possibility of a blow-up. However, if dating after marriage were acceptable to her, her husband, and her community, it would offer an option heretofore excluded. And in that regard, it is important to realize that community need not mean the whole blooming town and everyone in it! It can often be enough if community means those friends and acquaintances whose opinion really matters. In that regard, there can be some latitude of choice. Shall we choose exclusive-possessive friends who would look askance at dating after marriage as an *a priori* evil? If we have such friends, they cannot be part of the inner circle in whom we confide about our dates. Could we not choose supportive peers who can see the advantages of dating after marriage and who, at the same time, are clear-headed and honest enough to alert us if the advantages seem to be overwhelmed by the risks? Meanwhile, of course, since dating after marriage does not give the *appearance* of sexual monogamy, though it may be so, in fact, the pro-dating community may need to cover and protect each other *vis-à-vis* the community at large.

Many people will eventually discover a supportive peer group, but with regard to dating after marriage, not a supportive spouse. That makes things more difficult, but not impossible. We will come to that later.

We believe that the decision to date or not to date should be up to each individual. We suggest that it be allowed to compete with other options on its own merits. Then let the statistics be gathered to give us an indication of how many of us need it, the kinds of instances in which it is viable, and the situations in which it is not.

Meanwhile, what right have the anti-daters to condemn dating out of hand without reliable evidence as to its value? If marriage is 70 or 80 percent good, should it be discarded because it is 30 percent or 20 percent flawed? But that is what is happening now.

We feel that making dating an individual decision would go a long way toward mollifying discontent and make marriages more viable. Not only that, but for many of us, if we could date openly—be it for escape pure and simple, or for comfort or to give a lonesome person a good time, or to add a new dimension to a couple-couple friendship—mightn't we be more honest, and a bit more zestful?

Dating after marriage is not really so far out. A large number of couples right now engage in a lifestyle that is equally unconventional— swinging. Both husband and wife attend the swinging parties and engage in third-party sex with the knowledge and often in the presence of the spouse. Many who swing say it has helped their marriages. We have no reason to doubt it. Nevertheless, it seems clear that swinging is an extention of the exclusive-possessive style of marriage, as in "we do *everything* together. The couple that swings together stays together." Dates with other swingers between parties are forbidden and emotional involvements are resented.

In contrast, dating after marriage is a nonpossessive, one-to-one relationship between two persons rather than merely between two sex objects. Dating means specifically that you want to be alone, to relate on a one-to-one basis without wondering whether or not your husband or wife is having a good time. A dating relationship may be primarily on an intellectual and emotional plane. It may include tenderness and comforting and even wild, wild fun—and still not sex. It is made to order for those who crave additional closeness and intimacy and who do not necessarily want to be involved in a situation programmed to lead inexorably into bed, as is the case with swinging and most behind-closed-doors affairs. Then, if dating leads to occasional explicit sex, it is more a matter of choice than of programming.

Dating after marriage is not programmed for sex or against it. Rather, it is programmed for freedom: freedom to touch, to exchange glances, to hold hands, to walk along the beach, to be emotional, to be involved, to discover another human being as a person in a context where both of you are free of the usual role requirements of wife, husband, parent, and so on.

And unlike the dating we typically do before marriage, dating after marriage is not a search for a permanent partner. Freed of the dating games we used to play, who knows how much fun dating might be?

We propose that the dating age no longer be considered a transitional time between puberty and marriage, but as a uniquely rewarding and ongoing way to relate to others. Escape? Comfort? Good Samaritan? An added dimension to a couple-couple friendship? All these, and more. Opening many dimensions closed to us before, dating after marriage might bring more durability to some marriages, provide a human touch for some who are lonely and, at the least, add a few fun experiences to our three score years and ten.

chapter 3

the myth of
the scarcity of love

Myth has several dictionary meanings. One meaning is that of a legendary story often about deities or demigods and the creation of the world. But when we use the word "myth" throughout this chapter, we are referring to a collective belief that reflects and is in response to the wishes of the group. This is the sociological meaning of myth.

Like many myths that are passed on from generation to generation without examination, logic is not the strong point of the myth of the scarcity of love.

This myth or collective belief refers to erotic love shared with more than one person. It does not apply to the amount of *eros* shared with your spouse or, during the more liberal past half century or so, with your one-to-one heterosexual love partner. Nor does it refer to nonerotic love shared with many different persons.

Both *caritas* (caring love of human concern) and *philia* (supportive love emphasizing loyalty) are regarded as relatively open-ended, able to be stretched to include additional persons without depleting the supply. They can be extended beyond one's spouse to include children, kin, fellow lodge members, and on and on.

Erotic love is regarded as the outcast. Within marriage, it is supposed to be practically limitless. But if you use up only half your capacity for erotic love among three different people, the amount used is considered a strain on your supply even though the other half of your supply remains unused.

The reality is that within variable limits, erotic love is self-perpetuating: the more you love, the greater is your capacity to love. In addition, different persons have different levels of erotic vitality, and this changes from time to time for any individual.

We believe that *philia* is potentially more problematical than *eros*. Loyalties often conflict. During the Civil War, loyalty to one's country often conflicted with loyalty to one's family, pitting father against son and brother against brother in the border states. Many people experience loyalty conflicts created by the differing values of their parents and their love partners.

We do not believe that the expression of erotic love for more than one person must be interpreted as an act of disloyalty in and of itself, or that extramarital eroticism must, by its nature, create divided loyalties. Erotic involvement with more than one person need not set the stage for loyalty conflicts, unless eroticism is limited to an exclusive commitment.

We find clear moral advantages in distinguishing between acts stemming from *philia, caritas,* and *eros*. When *caritas* is not lumped with *philia,* especially in its extreme form of unwavering allegiance, persons can extend their circles of caring. We all understand that a gift of food to a hungry person does not imply a lifelong commitment of support. If it did, charity would cease, or many of us would be burdened beyond our means.

In like manner, when *eros* is not inextricably lumped together with *philia,* it is possible to enjoy sexuality with additional partners without conflicting loyalties. It should be clearly stated that the erotic involvement is for the moment and is not an act of commitment. Again it must be emphasized that we are not denigrating those who are able to combine *eros, caritas,* and *philia* in a single relationship.

We are aware that some conservative moralists will regard genital sexuality as acceptable only within the context of a lifelong commitment. We recognize that many persons, especially women, have been burned by mistakenly regarding a sexual act as an implied commitment. Before contraception was universally available, sexuality was accompanied by the spectre of pregnancy with its economic and social consequences. Men were also trapped into unwanted commitments via the shotgun wedding.

Traditional marriage had well established standards long before the era of contraception, urbanization, and affluence. According to these standards, whatever erotic love cannot be shared with one's spouse must be denied. Ideally each marriage partner has the same amount of libido and channels all of it into the marriage relationship. Frustration of *eros* has been an accepted part of married life for the countless married persons for whom this ideal was not true. Extramarital sex is traditionally regarded as irresponsible *ipso facto*. Considering the risk of unwanted pregnancy, it often was irresponsible, but the tradition no longer fits the realities.

Although it may be ideal to combine sexuality and loving concern with lifelong loyalty, there are countless persons in our society who are in desperate need of warm human touches but who are in no realistic position to make a social or economic commitment.

In addition there are many others who because of physical or mental handicaps will probably never find sex or love, if love, sex, and commitment are forcibly inseparable. It is our educated guess that a significant number of these unfortunate persons—some mentally handicapped, some scarred by burns or crippled or palsied, some handicapped by intense fear and anxiety, some physically trapped in institutions— have not been able to attract a love partner.

People are so afraid to get trapped by the desperate need of deprived persons that they do not offer to touch at all. And deprived persons are so afraid of rejection, even more so than the rest of us, that they dare not reach out. Warm messages about love are everywhere, but these persons are left out in the cold.

We suggest that a study be made of the possible benefits of temporary love, love games, and eroticism for these very human persons in need of one-to-one adult human love and sex. But of course, so long as we insist that eroticism and lifelong commitment must go hand in hand, such persons must continue to be excluded from the circle.

We know from personal experience with groups that when commitment is clearly limited, persons are able to reach out to a less attractive person and give warm human caresses that would be impossible under normal social conditions.

To add to the list are those institutionalized married persons in love with their spouses but denied the opportunity to make love because our antiquated system demands that all patients, prisoners, and other institutionalized persons suppress erotic needs for the duration of their stay. Anyone who demonstrates an otherwise normal sex drive runs the risk of being labeled a sex maniac: "How dare you have sexual feelings when you are in a hospital, nursing home, prison, mental institution?" And add to these the frightened loners outside institutions, loners who cannot compete for the prize and who haven't the capacity to break the rules and find imperfect, uncommitted love.

For those who are not institutionalized, the myth continues to make marriage an exception. One message within the myth of the scarcity of love is that everyone has a specific amount of erotic love that is irreplaceable. If you use it up when you are young, you will have less when you are old. If you use it up on many relationships, you will have less left for your primary relationship. Only in marriage, according to the popular belief, is it true that the more you love, the greater capacity you develop.

Outside of marriage, according to the myth, one must guard one's supply of erotic love for fear of wasting some precious eroticism that will be needed in marriage. But inside marriage, the more you use your supply of *eros*, the greater the supply will become!

Thus, tradition has demanded that erotic love and exclusive commitment be cemented together. But the limits of time and energy are in fact quite different from the limits of eroticism. It is true that for many persons, having a lover in addition to one's spouse turns out to be disastrous. Standard marriage texts, articles, and mass media repeatedly make this point. Our point is that erotic love with another partner does not necessarily destroy a primary relationship; that there is nothing inherent in the dynamics of eroticism that requires a single object of expression; that sharing eroticism may be destructive or beneficial depending on capacities, attitudes, and sensitivity to the needs of the partners and not dependent on the myth that giving to one partner necessarily and always takes away from the other.

To repeat the point made by psychologist Marshall Bryant Hodge, ". . . a marriage often survives extramarital affairs. In fact, it may be strengthened as the result of a new-found ability to be open to the experience and expression of love."

Like many popular myths, the myth of the scarcity of love relies on several premises, each of which builds upon the preceding premise as long as no one questions the basic assumptions. These premises are:

1. Erotic love is a magic process that makes everything right. To be unloved is to be incomplete. To prove that one is not incomplete, one must find love. This in itself sells lots of shampoo, deodorant, mouth wash, and after-shave lotion.

Now it might seem that such love would be readily available, for there are plenty of reasonably attractive people around, all of whom need love and know how to say nice things, kiss, give strokes, and so on.

2. However, to be magically potent, love must be the right kind— not only the love itself—but its source must also be right. It must come from the right kind of person, a person whose looks, accomplishments, prestige, age, potential ("He's a pre-med, Mommie!"), etc., make the love right. Such love will turn the toad into a prince, awaken the Sleeping Beauty inside us, and transport Cinderella to the castle on Prince Charming's arm. Such love and only such love.

Granted that sometimes the right person does not evoke the right love in you, there would seem to be more than enough right people around who would indeed send out right vibes and make you feel the right love.

3. To be right, this love must also be exclusive. It is not available from a person who already loves someone else! Each princess

has but one kiss with which to transform a single toad and must save her real kiss until she finds that toad. By the same token, each prince has a single glass slipper to fit only the Cinderella destined to share his castle. Given the diversity of female feet, that limits the field somewhat. To mix fairy tales, when at last Cinderella finds her prince-toad, they get married. The slipper fits and the warts are woven into princely robes and that is that.

So there you are. You must find love or be incomplete. It must come from the right person and it must also be exclusive. So you save up your love, don't use or receive any, so that you will be prepared when it suddenly appears. You may be warm and affectionate while looking for it, but no eroticism, please! So you search and search, feeling miserable in your incompleteness. You may be caught up in new interpretations of what's right for men and women. If you are female and interested in being a crane operator, there won't in the foreseeable future be many males who will include you in their search for the right person. If you are male and a ballet dancer, you may learn that dancers are seldom found on the Mr. Right lists of women.

But most of us have less obvious difficulties. More likely you are wandering around in the marketplace for a particular kind of person with attributes that appear to be moderately plentiful. But, although other kinds of love can be exchanged regardless of physical size, attractiveness, racial background, age, sex, and marital status, in erotic love you must find a match. And it is even better if you can match higher than yourself, for there is a standard set by society that is used to measure how well you did in your game of search and seizure.

By far the most important item is physical appearance. Wow, if you can catch a partner who is better looking than you, you get lots of strokes. We can say that these strokes are irrational and unfair and probably be right, but the reality is that if you are only so-so attractive and are engaged to a beautiful or handsome person, you do in fact get strokes that make you feel good. Parading around your applause-getting partner is a real top-of-the-world kind of experience. No matter what happens, no one can take those moments of glory away from you. Looks do count.

If you can't get one better, at least get one as sexually attractive as you are, i.e. your own perception of yourself. It is downright humiliating to be identified with someone who is much lower on the sex-appeal ladder than you are. "Couldn't you do better than *that?*" comes through loud and clear as everyone is shaking hands, smiling, and politely responding to their introduction to your new friend. In spite of the fact that he or she is kind, understanding, lovable, very smart, professionally competent, has the right family background, you never really get to know that person. You keep on saying to yourself just what you've been taught, "looks don't count," but you don't return his or her call.

In general, looks do count. But in individual cases, each of us has the potential to buck the system. A short man can marry a tall woman but they have to have a lot more going for them than the outwardly suited couple with all kinds of societal support. The same is true of so-called mixed marriages, whether it is race, religion, age difference, social status, or physical appearance. When you make a good match, you can draw on a huge support system to help you cement the relationship. When you insist on an odd combination, society can hardly wait to prove that you made a mistake. Then people say, "I told you so" to mix-match couples, to the tall and the short; to the beautiful and the plain; to the black and the white; to the rich and the poor; to the fundamentalist and the atheist; to the young and the old; to the bright and the dull; to the conservative and the radical. In fact, for the radical and the radical, even matching won't help them.

Clearly we have added other marks of acceptability to the original looks factor. But together they make up the appearance bag. How do you present yourselves to others? Do other people approve of your partner; your family, your colleagues, your friends?

Big Ben and Little Louis were in the locker room shower together one day. Big Ben, who had an unusually large cock, said to Little Louis, who had a very small one:

"Say, do you enjoy sex?"

"Why sure," said Little Louis, "I love screwing a lot. Wow, you must have a ball with all that going for you."

"You mean you don't have any trouble getting it up and keeping it up for a good long play time?" said Big Ben.

"Hell, no", said Louis, "I haven't got much, but I keep in good training . . . gotta make the most of what you have."

"Oh," replied Ben.

"But why the questions? How about you, Ben?" quipped Louis.

"How would you like to trade one that works for one that looks good in the shower!" yelled Ben.

But don't dismiss the fairy tale approach lightly. In the fairy tale, Princes and Princesses are surrounded by magic; they are not only beautiful, but loving and capable, each making everything right for the other. And our muddled middle-class messages to children encourage and support this: everything changes when the right person comes into your life. Do we not indeed teach little boys that ordinary girls are there to please and serve them; are toys to play with; are temptresses to be avoided—all except the magic one, the one who is to be loved and respected forever? And do we not tell little girls that boys are bad, always thinking of themselves; that they will use you for selfish gratification, except that one magic boy who will cherish you forever? Moreover we also tell girls that they themselves are bad, at least their genitalia are. Genitalia are never to be discovered, examined, or played with, or even talked about in positive terms. In effect, we say to little girls, "Sex is dirty, save it for the one you love!" And then the genital area which used to be dirty suddenly becomes clean and beautiful, deserving of loving caresses. Is that really so different from the glass slipper of Cinderella?

When you are facing life either before finding your right love or are living in a period where your right love is either absent or inadequate, you are denied lesser loves, for there is only one glass slipper for each person—so you save, hoard, guard, and withhold erotic love from all others. If the princess kisses another, the prince returns to his toadlike state. Beauty resumes her sleeping, pumpkin carriages arrive, and the castle crumbles.

The message is: Since I may not be completely right for you, I dare not ask for love because rejection is so painful. I am to suppress erotic love feelings until I am quite sure I can meet all the demands of my potential partner and have all my demands met by him or her.

Such exclusive use of erotic loves precludes any number of incomplete but pleasure-filled love experiences. Certainly it precludes the playing of love games and the use of humor in regard to erotic love. The idea of playing with love is a travesty of all we have been told to hold sacred.

Whenever people treat erotic love lightly, we only hear about the bad effects, the exploitations, the hurts. We are not allowed to know about the people who make a clear contract for temporary love and each partner has a positive experience. Suppose you and your friend decide to play being in love tonight. You love your date, now, tonight; but you do not want a future commitment; you feel the need to love and be loved, but you do not want to enter into an exclusive pair-bond or, perhaps, you do not want to destroy an existing enduring pair-bond.

In a rational setting, one might be able to communicate such very real feelings, but as of this writing, blunt honesty in dealing with how one feels about love is discouraged.

Sometimes the need to love or be loved may not include explicit sex. Perhaps it would mean an evening of romantic doings—walking along a path holding hands, exchanging glances and loving phrases that we have been warned to save for that one moment. Of course, there is a risk that what started out as fun might conceivably end up hurting someone. But to deny this fun to everyone at all times because some people will misuse it sometimes is like denying cars because of accidents, pastry because of obesity, wine because of alcoholism, and on and on.

If we could legitimize other forms of love, we could help people enjoy nonexclusive relationships without getting hurt. We could work diligently on guidelines, starting with making a clear contract and remaining sensitive to the needs of the other.

Moreover, played as we perceive them, these games are only partly pretend. They do ignore the usual implications of the in-love behavior, but they may express very real here and now feelings—especially the need to love and be loved, even if only for a moment, and even if it doesn't matter a great deal with whom!

We recall a short story about a lonely sailor leaving the next morning for overseas duty. He searched for a loving soulmate. He wanted to hold a woman close, to be tender and sentimental, to be in love for his last night in this country. He wasn't too handsome and certainly not sophisticated and was having no luck at all with the relatively few girls around, when an older woman appeared on the scene. They talked. She was so kind. She listened. She understood. She was not at all aggressive, just compassionate. He wanted so much to hold her in his arms, feel the warmth of skin to skin contact, gently caress a female body and mostly to feel close to someone. She understood that too and they went to bed together. The story goes on to relate how much that night meant to him and how rare it was to feel so comfortable in such a socially awkward situation.

What he wanted was a mother, some will say and demand that the behavior be labeled as sick. We say that to limit warm rewarding human contacts to specified ages, sexes, or future commitments is to prejudge irrationally what human values are all about. A positive experience for two persons does not become negative because of age or lack of long term commitment. But our myths picture such temporary love as dastardly and evil—surely the wicked witch will punish such behavior!

Many marriage experts say that despite the importance of whom one marries, many marriages actually happen because of the need to marry at that time, and whoever came along would be seen in a very different light a few years either before or after. All the socioeconomic reasons to get married fall into the category of what status you seek, and while you are seeking that status, you may settle for persons that would not have appeared as the right person had you met that person at a different time in your life. Nevertheless, even with all this knowledge and background about non-Cinderella love, we continue to pretend that temporary, noncommitted love is bad, worse than no love at all. The message that erotic love is magical, unique, and destined for one person only is what we still hear, but how many of us believe it?

Cornelia has lived through two pair-bond relationships, one going steady without coitus, and one live-in arrangement that recently ended. She is now unattached and dates several men. Tonight she feels lonely, frustrated, and wants to make love. Unlike the sailor, she doesn't want to go to the bar and pick up someone she doesn't know, but between two of her friends, Don and Ted, she honestly doesn't have a strong preference; whichever one is in the mood is okay with her. Traditional society says that this is not a valid feeling; that Cornelia is bad; that psychologically healthy young women want to make love only if they are committed to an exclusive relationship. The experts will cite examples from psychiatrists' files about all their Cornelia-type patients, with no control group of women who did not become disturbed and seek help.

Cornelia may or may not regret her decision. And please do not conclude that we believe all girls are potential Cornelias or that Cornelia's lifestyle is to be promoted. Not at all, but we do believe that Cornelia has a right to exist with dignity; that her feelings are real and to be accepted. We make a clear distinction between accepting feelings and accepting the acting out of feelings. We firmly believe in limitations to the acting out of feelings, especially if they will hurt others. But we deplore the putting down of the Cornelias for their honest and warm sexual feelings for more than one partner.

As we have said before, this book is about sophisticated, affluent, mobile persons living in an urban setting. We fully understand how traditional attitudes developed. We acknowledge that traditional marriages were made for economic necessity, that women were regarded as property, not even allowed to own their own property, not able to vote, and that marriage was a social unit making two persons whole and fit for society. What we are demanding is the right to examine the myths about erotic love that we have inherited. The myths may have served a purpose at one time, but we believe that now they are perpetuated as scientific truth without the support of rational evaluation. The result, in our opinion, is a restrictive view of eroticism that condemns many persons to lives of desperate loneliness and some to lack of any type of erotic love whatsoever.

We resent the traditional insistence that only those committed to a particular person are allowed to experience erotic love. We deplore that to have an open-ended need for eroticism that could be filled by any of several, or many, persons without commitment is regarded as wrong, bad, neurotic, exploitive (for males), and cheap (for females). Why must we condemn people for honest feelings? Most teen-age boys have sexual needs and would like to have sex without lifetime commitment. Many single women are lonely and would like warmth, loving, closeness, and/or coitus without having to make a life-long decision. When it comes to eroticism society demands that you find the right person first before you can legitimately express or fulfill your needs.

We tend to apply the all-or-none law only to eroticism. Other positive sensual experiences such as eating and listening to music are legitimately enjoyed at various levels, without condemning the less-than-ideal. For instance, no one condemns popular musicals because they are not as high quality as opera; no one denies the enjoyment of a backyard barbeque even though it is not as discriminating as a gourmet banquet. Despite the obvious differences, eroticism does have a certain commonality with music and food: all three can be enjoyed in varying forms, for various reasons and in different degrees of perfection.

With the advent of free time, effective contraception, antibiotics and legal abortion, the feasibility of responsible eroticism outside of marriage has increased radically, while our pronouncements about the evils of all extramarital erotic experiences have lingered on. The result is that unnecessary guilt and anxiety often haunt the less sophisticated; that tremendous conflicts arise in those who see the irrationality of traditional thinking, but have no support in their particular community for a more humane approach to sex. Hopefully, this book will help sanction an investigation of attitudes toward human sexuality without promoting any one rigid dogma.

Two points we feel compelled to repeat throughout the book: first, no put-down is intended for those who live happily within the limits of an exclusive relationship and second, that reaching out does indeed incur risks. We are writing about, a subject that is portrayed in many books, heavily biased in favor of limiting erotic love to one partner. Persons who do indeed have successful traditional marriages need no additional support: their families, their clergymen, their communities, their bosses, everyone offers them support. We are trying to promote the concept that there are other ways of looking at romance and marriage. We ask you to consider nonexclusive love as an option, not a second choice for those who fail to reach the ideal.

If limited love were accepted as a valid human interaction, we believe many more persons would dare to love. For those unable to find partners, we believe there are available givers of such love, providing they are assured of restricted commitment. We are in the process of studying receivers. We are learning about how many and in what ways intimacy-deprived persons would like caring, loving, touching in a limited, somewhat structured way. We joy in the fantasy of Love Night in institutions, when everyone who chooses to participate will have a love partner for the evening. Some will accuse us of promoting promiscuity. We hope you understand and will enlighten them. Love is a many splendored thing.

Thus, one aspect of the myth of the scarcity of erotic love involves the application of the all-or-none law. In other words, erotic love is scarce only when outside an exclusive relationship; within the relationship it is infinite. Also there are the strong messages about good and bad. Within the exclusive relationship, it is very, very good, and outside the relationship, it is very, very bad. This may be called the romantic exclusive side supporting the scarcity theory for everyone outside the primary bond. But the myth also has a side that is no more romantic than balancing one's checkbook. The nonromantic assumptions of the myth of the scarcity of love include:

1. Each of us has only a certain, fixed amount of love to give, spend, or sell.
2. If this amount is divided among several people, each of them gets less. If someone who loves me loves others, I will get less.
3. Love can be saved.
4. If I've saved all my love for you, and you haven't saved all yours for me, I'm getting a raw deal.

The basic fault in these assumptions is the view that love is parallel to an economic commodity—in fact a nonrenewable resource! We refuse to use the knowledge of how erotic love reinforces itself and grows within a primary relationship and apply it to the dynamics involved in other erotic experiences. Outside the primary relationship we pretend that erotic love takes on totally new characteristics, namely, those of limited and fixed supply.

Actually, love is a physiological and emotional process, and as such can never be saved. To do so is like lying in bed for years saving one's muscles for the Olympics! There is, of course, no way to hoard or save love, though many people pretend they can do it. What in fact happens is that one simply acts unloving until the proper opportunity for loving comes along, by which time one may have lost the capacity through disuse.

The myth of the scarcity of love irrationally holds that erotic love is scarce and that the thing to do is hoard it and guard our resources. The net effect of this is to make love scarce. For everywhere, there are human beings surrounded by other people and, let us assume, all of them are looking for love. Sally and Pete are saving their love for somebody else—that is, they are acting unloving and feeling virtuous about it. Rich is rather like General Jack D. Ripper in the film *Dr. Strangelove.* He is afraid of losing some of his "precious bodily fluids," which, he thinks, are the source of his hard-driving success. He doles out the fluids twice monthly to his wife. Annie wants some love, like a backrub, but not sex—and she's afraid that if she shows the warm affection she feels for Tom he will misinterpret it as a sexual come-on. Tom, meanwhile, guards his warm feelings, for since love is scarce, he doesn't want to alert the scarce resources (Annie) to the fact that the hunter is near. And Angela does not believe in a fixed amount of love and she wants to relate lovingly with whomever she trusts and likes, with or without sex, but she doesn't know how to communicate this. So all of them are looking for love, and all of them could give it, and all of them go without it, which proves once again what they all knew all along: love is scarce!

Thus, the myth of the scarcity of love, in its exclusive romantic, and in its calculated miserly aspects, has affected our loving for the worse. As Philip Slater observed in *The Pursuit of Loneliness:*

> If one assumes scarcity, then the knowledge that others want the same things that we have leads . . . to preparations for defense, and, ultimately (since the best defense is offense), for attack. The same assumption leads to a high value placed on the ability to postpone gratification (since there is not enough to go around). The expression of feelings is a luxury, since it might alert the scarce resources that the hunter is near.

But the myth of the scarcity of love will not be overturned in a day. For one thing, almost all of us have experienced the scarcity of love as have Sally, Pete, Rich, Annie, Tom, and Angela. But even more significantly, most of us were reared in small family units of one or two parents with children. Love and censure came almost exclusively from at the most two adults, especially in our first three to five years.

Generations ago children were reared in a permanent home with an extended family. Different types of love were experienced within the family in an established and predictable way. But in our highly technological mobile society, children find themselves in a family unit that consists only of themselves and one or two parents. Each relationship within this tiny unit is intensified because there are no other persons within the unit to absorb some of the emotional heat. Of course this is a great oversimplification, and many readers will rightfully think how horrible it was with grandmother living with us and how great it was when she left. But the chances are that grandmother was uprooted from her friends and surroundings and planted within a bustling, youth-oriented, small home. We do not intend to discuss the advantages and disadvantages of the extended family here, however.

To oversimplify, Freudians tend to view the source of adult jealousy as the child's battle for the attention of the other-sexed parent, a battle, as it were, against the same-sexed parent. Little boys unconsciously want Daddy out of the way so they can have Mommy to themselves, and little girls would liquidate Mommy in order to have Daddy.

But whether or not we believe the Freudian model, our family setup is exclusivist. The child's perception must be: "When I need love (guidance, help, approval, food, backrubs, a shoulder to cry on) just one or two people are typically available." Other relationships, such as to teachers and relatives (including grandparents) are intermittent and less significant.

If these two parents, or in many cases, only one, convey to the child a dependable and consistent experience of being loved and respected, the child is likely to feel more secure.

Yet at the same time, and as part of the secure experience, the child learns a terrible vulnerability. To draw an analogy from financial investments, the child's portfolio of emotional stocks is not diversified—90 percent or more of his stocks are in two companies, often in just one. If the parents pay high emotional dividends, he is an emotional millionaire. But if they don't, he may be wiped out. Even when his stocks are doing very well, he is aware from experience of the likelihood of bad quarters—illnesses, preoccupation or absence of the parents—with few dividends. He is also aware that great depressions are a possibility: "How come Johnny's Mommy and Daddy got divorced? Are you going to get divorced?" Or, "Susie's Mommy died. You aren't going to die, are you?" These anxieties are realistic. The vulnerability is there.

How much healthier for the child and for the involved adults if closeness, loyalty, love, and warmth could be extended to more people. There are lots of single persons—never-marrieds, divorced adults, widows and widowers—who would appreciate a deep meaningful relationship with one or more children, without taking on the full emotional and financial responsibility of rearing a child. With our mobile society, it does mean learning to love and let go; developing intimacy with the realistic expectation that it may not last. Again we are confronted with our all-or-none concepts. Of course it hurts to leave someone you love, but does it hurt less than those same years with no love relationship at all? And the relationship does not have to disappear entirely because there is a physical distance in between. What a good feeling for a child to know that those letters come from someone he or she knows and cares deeply about; someone who would respond if the need were great; someone to visit sometime in the future. Why not diversify the stocks?

But we are trained not to risk love with new acquaintances. True stories of how persons were ripped off, hurt, and destroyed by such trusting are easy to come by. So millions of parents go through weekly routines, never with a whole day off, and other millions of singles, young and old, go for weeks without feeling someone really needs them. And our culture, with all its technology, makes little or no attempt to get the two groups together. And the child, the center of the discussion, actually, keeps his or her vulnerability, limiting his or her portfolio to one or two stock companies.

Possessive jealousy emerges from this experience of a limited portfolio of emotional stocks. And reinforcing the experience that the sources of love are limited is the model. The model is how children see the ways in which adults live. What they typically see is the exclusive male-female pair. At least, it appears to be exclusive! This is observed as the acknowledged, acceptable source of love among adults. The model programs children to become half of just such an exclusive diad—to enter into the traditional, sexually monogamous marriage. The same model sows the seeds of self-doubt and even shame or guilt about not becoming half of an exclusive pairing.

As if this were not enough, the model of the exclusive pair also demonstrates that marriage is a status performance. It is the only real rite of passage we have left to recognize and to celebrate the transition from child status to adult status! Except, perhaps, among those for whom religious confirmations are seriously taken as a transition to adulthood. Marriage is how one becomes unmistakably a member of the adult community. Smoking cigarettes doesn't really do the job. Joining the Army or getting pregnant come closer. But marriage is the real thing.

Now, when being married becomes part of one's adult status, threats to this status are keenly felt. To be a married person is felt as being somehow higher than to be an old maid, an eccentric bachelor, a homosexual, or a divorced woman, though these states are continuously becoming more acceptable. Currently there is less stigma to being single, or divorced, than even a generation ago. There are many dynamics involved. One certainly is in the movement to afford individuals more rights irrespective of how tradition defines their status. Another is the women's liberation movement that is related, but not identical. Females are getting closer to being accepted as persons rather than each one as a "wife of" someone else.

Another dynamic operating in many marriages is the concept of territorial imperative. Man, like other creatures, guards his territory—his home, his turf, his homeland. Territory is often felt to include the spouse, especially for men.

We believe this imperative, however significant it is now, would be much less commanding if we could modify the other contributors to possessive feelings. These are, to review:

1.   The myth of the scarcity of love.
2.   The experience that the resources of love are limited—the emotional portfolio in which 90 percent of a child's stock is with just two companies: Mommy and Daddy. And increasingly, just one company. But, if his stocks are losers, can the child sell and buy others?
3.   The model of the exclusive male-female pair as the sole source of adult romantic and sexual affirmation.
4.   The personal status associated with marriage.
5.   The advantages of marriage in our pro-marital society—every-

thing from the privilege of a joint tax return and lower insurance premiums to the home, circle of friends, and community status that the Joneses share with each other.

Compartment Four marriage does not threaten the personal, social, and legal advantages of marriage. But it does recognize that the myth of the scarcity of love is a myth. Compartment Four marriage means adding true privacy to that time which is already spent on yourself as a person. Each marriage partner has a specified amount of time not spent with the job or family complex. When persons are extremely busy, possibly with small children, the amount of time may be very small. At another stage in the marriage, such time might add up to twenty hours a week or even more. We are discussing time for sports, for music, for art, for any hobby or activity that you do not share with your spouse. What Compartment Four does is to cut the strings; you are on your own. You decide what you want to do with this time. You are limited by your own conscience and your own sense of obligation, not your spouse's! Since your recreation time is your own, make it totally your own, and allow it to be evaluated on the basis of what it does for you.

This kind of marriage becomes possible when we recognize that the possessive jealousy most of us feel has its roots in childhood, the terrible vulnerability of having relied on one or two people for all the love we need. As children, there was no choice. But now, we are no longer children and we can make adult decisions. Why erotic love with just one person? Why limit outside love or friendship to those with no potential as sex partners? Do other loves really deplete the love available in marriage? If love is a physiological, emotional, even a muscular process, is one's capacity to be loving at home truly increased by repressing it with everyone else? If you are a male over sixty and going home in ten minutes to make love to your spouse, maybe. But if you are going to be away for two days or a week?

But what about the danger of "getting emotionally involved" outside one's marriage? First, such involvement can and does occur without explicit sex or even mutual recognition of any kind of "love." Second, for those who believe in the myth of scarcity of love, the danger of depleting one's pair-bond love is real. It is real because, in the myth, true love is limited and exclusive. You love your spouse or your lover. There is no such thing as positive lesser love. You cannot love your lover some and your spouse very much; you cannot love your lover very much and your spouse warmly and comfortably. You cannot, but what if you do?

Compartment Four marriage does not force you to face such dilemmas. For it is based on the premise that human beings can and do love more than one person at a time, differently perhaps, with more intensity here and more comforting there, sexually in one instance, and with complete honesty in another. As one loves different children, one may love different adults, and none need be exclusive.

When it comes to loving our children, we easily accept and indeed, we insist that our love is not exclusive. If a mother or father were to say, "I love Timmy," adding "and I love my other children too!" the exclusivist retort would be "How dare you say you love your other children when you just said you love Timmy?"

But we love Timmy for his spunk and determination, and another for his whimsy and winsome shyness, and a third for her helpful and sensible ways. One may even love them just for being themselves, no strings attached, which is a very nice kind of love to give and receive.

Yet when it comes to loving adults, one says, "Oh, but that's a different matter altogether." No, it isn't all that different; we simply allow ourselves to hug and love children more freely because it isn't sexual. The authors do not buy the clear distinction between erotic love and caring love. We know that many have erotic feelings toward siblings, children, and other safe relatives that we are allowed to touch and kiss. We know that very often what physically and socially passes for caring love includes transient, and sometimes deep, erotic feelings. By denying eroticism in our feelings toward our children, we can justify our insistence that we must love all sorts of different personalities in children. In fact we allow persons to love all different personalities in adults so long as there is no eroticism involved. But if there is even the slightest chance of the relationship being sexual, then our capacity to love more than one person is denied, or at least condemned! Other loves may be shared, but *eros,* according to the myth, is not to be shared. It comes in a fixed quantity and is to be isolated from the generous and giving aspects of caring love.

Clearly, Compartment Four marriage contradicts the myth and affirms the positive value of extramarital love for some people. This kind of marriage provides a framework in which extramarital love (with or without coitus) can supplement and enhance marital love. Partners in the ideal marriage learn how to cherish and care deeply about one another, without jealously guarding and limiting the freedom of each other to reach out and love others. For does the prisoner love the jailer?

In that regard, in a booklet entitled *Towards a Quaker View of Sex*, this statement was made: "The man who swallows the words 'I love you' when he meets another woman, may in that moment and for that reason begin to resent his wife's existence."

Compartment Four marriage does not require us to turn ourselves down every time we feel love. And whereas traditional marriage sees relationships as either-or, a marriage with a special compartment accepts relationships within realistic limits of energy and time. It provides a home but not a prison. It affirms that there may well be times when expressing extramarital love will not conflict with responsibility and sensitivity to the needs of those at home.

We feel that this kind of marriage is in some ways more hard-headed and realistic, less miserly and more optimistic, than the myth of the scarcity of love. In Compartment Four marriage:

1. Love is not a magic process that makes everything right. Love is a creative activity engaged in by people who reach out to build loving relationships.

2. People to love are anywhere and everywhere. No single prince is looking for me, carrying my glass slipper. The people one could love and be loved by are many and diverse.

3. To be valuable, love need not be exclusive. Persons with a great capacity for love might create temporary love ties with many others over a period of time without shortchanging anyone.

4. No one has a fixed amount of love. Loving is a physiological and emotional process which, like athletic skill, increases with practice. There is a limit, of course. But the limit is set by time and energy, not by the nature of love itself.

5. Love cannot be saved. To attempt to do so would be like wearing a blindfold to save your sight.

6.   If you have been saving your love for me, you have been getting a lot of practice in acting unloving and repressing your positive feelings, which may mean that I'm about to be loved poorly.
7.   To love is to risk, to make oneself vulnerable to real hurt. But not to love is also to risk and makes one vulnerable to the pain of loneliness and repression. To be fully informed, to be rational about consequences, and to be honest about your own feelings is to take the least risk.

How do these assumptions operate in a situation when you meet a new person and feel a warm, glowing response to him or her? Do you enjoy the glow and reach out or do you deny it and back away? There may be practical reasons for backing away, even for those with Compartment Four marriages—obligations at home, for example.

These contrasts are somewhat overdrawn, but in general, exclusive-possessive people view spontaneous attractions as threatening, for they might lead to something. Thus, the exclusive-possessive person is not free to explore new relationships fully, especially those relationships that would appear most promising from the point of view of additional warmth, closeness, and love. We must save, guard, and hoard, for the paradox emerges that the more you think you might like someone, the more you must avoid him.

Adults who use their ability to make decisions in many matters in life often suddenly feel threatened by a decision relating to any intimacy outside the pair-bond. Instead of thinking rationally about actual consequences, they tend to ignore percentages and try, at all costs, to avoid any risk at all. They regard sex and/or emotional disaster as an inevitable consequence instead of being open about how the relationship might progress.

In contrast, nonpossessive people with Compartment Four marriages also realize that the glow of positive response might lead to something, but they want to find out what. They want to enjoy the glow they feel and, if feasible, build on it. Whatever limits they set are realistic ones, such as lack of inclination, time, or energy, and these are evaluated in a logical fashion. In that regard, mistakes are made, but one is also free to learn from the mistakes. And at the least, the nonpossessive person can openly express the warm feelings, even when it's not realistically possible to do much about them. Doing something doesn't necessarily mean sex. There is a difference between sexual freedom and sexual compulsiveness!

Thus, spontaneous feelings of attraction can be explored. Might there be friendship? Intellectual stimulation? Sex? Whatever might evolve, nonpossessive people do not habitually regard their positive intuitive responses as temptations to be suppressed, but rather as open options that may turn out to be joys or bummers.

But for those who believe that true love is exclusive and limited, any warm, and especially sexual, urge toward an adult third party must be viewed as challenging the validity of the exclusive love to which one is already committed. And by the same token, a spouse's warm feelings toward adult third parties invalidate the established marital vow. This incites possessive jealousy and a fear of losing love, of being abandoned. For after all, if love must be exclusive, to love someone else requires abandonment. Hence, a tendency to cling to those whom one loves, or, more properly, to cling to the one, the one and only, with whom you share love.

In that regard, we offer you an illustrative story, an adaptation of "A Fairytale" by psychologist Claude M. Steiner.

Once upon a time, there lived two very happy people called Tim and Maggie with two children called John and Lucy.

To understand how happy they were, you have to understand how things were in those days. For you see, in those days everyone was given at birth a small, soft fuzzy bag. And anytime a person reached into his bag he was able to pull out a Warm Fuzzy.

As soon as the Fuzzy saw the light of day, it would smile and blossom into a large, shaggy Warm Fuzzy. You then would lay it on your shoulder or head or lap, and it would snuggle up and melt right against your skin and make you feel good all over. And if you wanted to feel good all over, you would just reach into your bag for a Warm Fuzzy and there it was!

But for some reason peculiar to the nature of Warm Fuzzies, the Warm Fuzzies other people gave you felt even warmer and fuzzier! In fact, twice as warm and fuzzy.

In those days, it was very easy to get Warm Fuzzies from other people. Anytime that somebody felt like it, he might walk up to you and say, "I'd like to have a Warm Fuzzy." There were always plenty to go around and so everyone felt warm and fuzzy most of the time.

But then one day the Bad Witch became angry because everyone was so happy and no one was buying her potions and salves. The Bad Witch was very clever and she devised a very wicked plan. One beautiful morning, she crept up to Tim and said, "See here, Tim, look at all the Warm Fuzzies that Maggie is giving to Lucy. You know, if she keeps it up, eventually she is going to run out and then there won't be any left for you."

Tim was astonished. He turned to the Witch and said, "Do you mean to tell me that there isn't a Warm Fuzzy in our bag every time we reach into it?"

And the Witch said, "No, absolutely not, and once you run out, that's it. You don't have any more!" With this she flew away on her broom.

Tim took the Witch's words to heart. He began to notice every time Maggie gave a Warm Fuzzy to somebody else. "What if she runs out?" he thought. "Then she won't have any left for me!" So Tim began to complain every time he saw Maggie give away a Warm Fuzzy, and because Maggie liked him very much, she stopped giving Warm Fuzzies away so often.

The children missed getting all the Warm Fuzzies Maggie used to give them. One day Lucy said, "Mommy, why don't you give me lots of Warm Fuzzies any more?"

"Because if I gave away too many, I might run out some day," Maggie told her.

"Will I run out too if I give Warm Fuzzies away?" Lucy asked.

"Absolutely," said Maggie. "And once you run out, that's it. You don't have any more!" With this, she picked up her broom and swept the floor.

Soon thereafter little John asked Lucy for a Warm Fuzzy.

"No," said Lucy, "because then I might run out. And once you run out, that's it. You don't have any more!"

And that made John very sad because he needed a Warm Fuzzy very much. But John took Lucy's words to heart, and stopped giving away Warm Fuzzies, too.

Before long, everyone felt worried about giving away too many Warm Fuzzies. "We might run out," everyone said, "and when you run out, that's it!"

So even though people still found Warm Fuzzies every time they

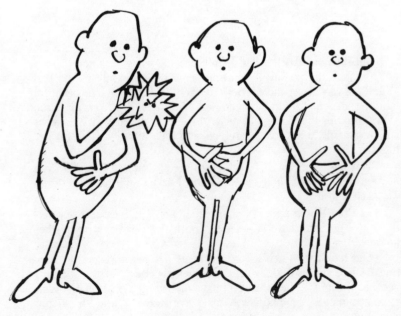

reached into their bags, they reached in less and less and became more and more stingy. At night, they hid their Fuzzy Bags under their pillows. They put locks on them and hid the keys. And when someone forgot where his key was, he couldn't even get out a Warm Fuzzy for himself!

And so Warm Fuzzies, which used to be as free as the air, became very scarce and very valuable. People who could not find a generous partner had to work long hours to earn money to buy Warm Fuzzies. Other people who were afraid of not being able to get Warm Fuzzies began to pair off and to reserve all their Warm Fuzzies for each other exclusively. Whenever one of the two persons forgot himself and gave a Warm Fuzzy to someone else, he would immediately feel terrible inside because he knew his partner would get mad and not let him have any Warm Fuzzies for a long time.

Another thing that happened was that when Warm Fuzzies were left in their bags too long they turned into Cold Pricklies, because that is what happens to Warm Fuzzies when they aren't used.

Then the Bad Witch opened a store where you could buy special plastic to cover Cold Pricklies and make them look like Warm Fuzzies. People thought they were getting Warm Fuzzies from each other, but they knew something was wrong when they started feeling cold and prickly. People became very confused about which fuzzies were real, and even the people who were still giving away real Warm Fuzzies were afraid of being cheated.

So things were very sad and dismal. And it all started because the Bad Witch made people believe that some day, when they least expected it, they might reach into their Warm Fuzzy Bag and find no more.

After a long, long time, a baby girl was born in a hidden valley where people had not heard of the Bad Witch and were not worried about running out of Warm Fuzzies. When the girl grew up, she wondered what was outside the valley. So one day she picked up her Warm Fuzzy Bag and walked over the hill.

When she got to the other side she saw people like she had never seen before. "My goodness," she thought, "they're all cold and prickly! They must need Warm Fuzzies!" So everywhere she went she kept reaching into her bag and giving away Warm Fuzzies. The children liked her very much because they felt good around her and they too began to give out Warm Fuzzies whenever they felt like it. Because they were young, their Warm Fuzzies had not had time to turn into Cold Pricklies.

One day, the Hip Woman (which they had begun to call her) met two Grown-Ups looking very sad and lonely.

"Have a Warm Fuzzy," she said.

"How do I know it's really a Warm Fuzzy?" one said.

"Try it and see," said the Hip Woman.

Then the Hip Woman came very close to the Grown-Ups and put a Warm Fuzzy on each lap. The Warm Fuzzies snuggled up and melted right against their skins and made them feel good all over. These were the first real Warm Fuzzies anyone had given them for a long time.

Afraid of losing their new Warm Fuzzies, the Grown-Ups put them into their Warm Fuzzy Bag, which, by now, were just full of old Cold Pricklies. After awhile, when they wanted to feel good again, a reach into the small bag would always produce a Warm Fuzzy. Lo and behold, most of the Cold Pricklies in the bags had turned back into Warm Fuzzies! So they went with the Hip Woman and gave away even more Warm Fuzzies than she did. The other Grown-Ups called them the Hip People.

Most of the Grown-Ups disapproved of the Hip People because they were giving the children the idea that they should not worry about running out of Warm Fuzzies.

But the Hip People and the children seemed not to care. Although the other Grown-Ups did all they could to stop them, the children went on giving away Warm Fuzzies whenever they felt like it. And because there were many children, it began to look as if they might have their way.

And don't be surprised if, along with the *caritas* and *philia,* you find *eros* in your own Warm Fuzzy Bag.

CHAPTER 4

COMPARTMENT FOUR

Dating after marriage and swinging are possible strategies for contemporary couples who want to enjoy romantic, intimate, and/or sexual relationships in addition to marriage. Open marriage is another option which, in principle, allows for extracurricular involvements.

But all three are limited in one basic regard that will rule them out for many of us. They require spousal agreement.

Therefore, many readers will perhaps feel that such opportunities for multiple intimacies sound good. But how do I get my spouse to agree?

Compartment Four marriage allows for independent decisions and does not require spousal agreement for every extramarital activity, whether the activity is intimate, sexual, or otherwise. This is true of any liberated relationships, be they friendships, live-in arrangements, or whatever.

Rather, the strategy of Compartment Four marriage is to structure time for each partner to act independently. It affirms that the couple share a life together—and at the same time, each life has a private sector. The decision for Compartment Four marriage is not a negative decision about honesty, but a positive one about privacy and freedom.

If you object to your partner opening your personal mail, or listening in on your telephone conversations, you should have little difficulty in understanding this principle. Even in traditional or open marriages, such activities are felt by most people to be invasions of privacy.

We take the position that persons are in fact far more individual, separate, private than those in love would like to project as their model. Perhaps in the height of in-loveness there is a span of time during which the following comments do not apply, but we believe for the vast majority of couples these exceptions to complete honesty and sharing are both true and desirable.

1. Personal mail—few adults want to be under pressure to share every piece of personal mail.
2. Personal telephone calls—few adults want to give full permission for their spouses to listen to any and all telephone conversations—how many would like to inform their friends that they cannot talk to you privately, everything they say may be overheard at random by another person?
3. Personal conversations—few adults would like to have their voices continually bugged, so that wherever they are, whatever

they say, could be heard by their spouse—complete with tone of voice and body language—you see, the bugging is with videotape.

4.	Fantasies—our videotape goes even further; every fantasy you have, no matter how destructive, how traumatic to your spouse, is recorded for instant replay—innocent fantasies about being single for a while, free to go off for a weekend, a week, a month (you are not seriously considering any of these, but the fantasies flash through the mind and are recorded) and fantasies during sex and about sex—every one, without exception, shared with your spouse in color and sound.

We admit this is an exaggeration without practical application, but we also believe it is helpful in understanding what Compartment Four is all about. The lack of privacy suggested above would make the authors feel less than human. As adults we want to relate to people without the obligation to report everything to our "other half," as some who promote togetherness like to call spouses.

Such degree of openness and sharing limits truly private conversations to spouses and singles! Being married then takes away an undue amount of personhood. One leaves the category of adult human being and becomes half of an institution. One does not have permission to think, decide, discuss, or act on one's own—for everything *must be able* to be reported—nothing, but nothing can be privately yours and yours alone . . . not even one secret feeling or fantasy, let alone a significant decision.

However, Compartment Four marriage extends the area of privacy to include not only mail, phone conversations, and so forth, but also a private compartment for outside activities. This private compartment, which is explicitly included in liberated marriage, is clearly marked personal. The spouse is not the One to whom all thoughts are open, from whom no secrets are hidden.

In traditional marriage, a private compartment is usually there, but it isn't always clearly marked private. It may include a dresser-drawer full of pictures of old beaux, a diary, or other personal items. It may include activities such as shooting pool with cronies that are sandwiched in between and hidden away among other activities. The problem is that when areas of privacy are not clearly marked "keep out," intrusions may take place by accident. The result can be great embarrassment, or much worse.

Our educated guess is that many couples hesitate to acknowledge such keep-out areas because they feel vaguely guilty about having them. Why? Perhaps because the keeping of secrets, the failure to share all activities, threatens the illusion of oneness which is the marriage ideal of so many people.

We believe that there is no rational reason to feel guilty about privacy. In the first place, almost every human relationship includes it, whether acknowledged or not. In the second place, to feel guilty about privacy is, in essence, to feel guilty about being human. For, after all, the only time any of us were really one with another person was when we were not quite persons at all, but a fetus in the womb of our mother.

But when the umbilical cord was cut, separateness was established and the journey toward autonomy began. Among other things, this process is one of individuation—learning to stand on one's own feet and make personal decisions. This process is not merely rewarding, but also painful. The nostalgia to achieve oneness again with another person is quite understandable, and this nostalgia has been structured into the popular mythology about marriage.

Sexual intimacy does indeed provide blissful moments when this oneness is almost an experiential reality, and this is one of the joys of sex for many people. However, it's irrational and useless to expect oneness twenty-four hours a day and in all aspects of living.

In our view, the freedom to relate, to tell, to touch, to share, or to refrain from doing so, characterizes adult relationships between equals. Compartment Four marriage openly affirms the private compartment of marriage for the sake of achieving an adult relationship between selves, rather than a regression to the dependencies of childhood or the oneness of the womb.

Traditionally, men have been able to continue their individuation while feeling very much "in love" and a high degree of "oneness" in the home aspects of life. With the female willing to be supportive and put the needs of her husband first, the MALE could count on his "love"

changing her schedule to fit his and being there when he wanted his "in-love" time. His partner for "oneness" was ready and waiting. But what if the "other half" of this in-love twosome also wants to pursue a career and refuses to wait back stage for the beck and call of her star performer? "Oneness" is much easier when you restrict the independence expectations of one marriage partner. We recognize that many persons, both male and female, do not want independence; that they *enjoy* the dependent role. Further, we hope that men will become liberated enough to declare their option to be dependent and will not suffer loss of dignity for electing the supportive role. But all that aside, this book is about those marriages in which both partners desire and agree to equal rights in personal decisions and fulfillment. We feel that acceptance of a person's private sector (C-4) is helpful for those who choose to continue the process of individuation after marriage.

However, it is important to explain that the Compartment Four concept is useful outside marriage as well. The life of a physician, for example, may be arbitrarily divided into three compartments:

Compartment One: The time the doctor spends in professional relationships with her patients. These include office visits and house calls, her hospital appearance in medical green, properly masked for the operating room ritual, the times when neighbors see her dashing for her car with little black bag in hand.

Compartment Two: Those times when the doctor is not with patients, but is doing things related to her medical practice. These include catching up on medical journals, attending professional meetings, shopping for new office equipment, talking with drug salesmen, attending refresher courses, and other similar activities.

Compartment Three: This includes everything the doctor does that is not related to her medical practice. Characteristic of Compartment Three activities are those that, were the general public or the doctor's patients to learn about them, would not interfere with their ability to see her as a doctor or weaken their confidence in her professional abilities. These activities could presumably include time spent with her family, vacations spent skiing or scuba diving, fixing the roof on the summer cottage, shopping for Christmas presents for her husband and children, and so on.

It is at this point that we would add another.

Compartment Four: This is a private area in the doctor's life, a time for which she is not accountable to the general public and, in particular, to her patients. The question may be asked, Why would a doctor want to do things she wouldn't want her patients to know about? Because a majority of people need to see their doctors as sober, concerned, wise, and fairly straight people in order to feel confidence in their professional abilities. Doctors live with a public image compounded of Ben Casey, Albert Schweitzer, Helen Tausig, Marcus Welby, and a Norman Rockwell painting of the old family doctor. Doctors are the scrubbed, sober ones in white coats, stethoscopes dangling, whose all-seeing eyes plumb the depths of one's infirmity with the acuity of an eagle spotting a distant mouse, swooping down with needles held aloft to vanquish the offending germs, or charging like St. George to slay the dragons in one's gut. This analogy is a bit overdrawn, but the fact remains that few of us want to be treated by a male doctor who likes to dress in women's clothes, who gets stoned with the janitor and his friends on Wednesdays and hosts sex orgies at the family summer cottage. In fact, most patients do not expect their doctors to be unconventional in any regard, including politics, religion, and overall lifestyle.

But increasingly now, we expect our doctors to be human up to and including an occasional fling. In other words, we like our doctors—and lawyers, and priests, and presidents—to be human, but not too human.

It is precisely at the point where one needs to be somewhat too human that Compartment Four is needed. It will include activities that will not in fact diminish one's ability to doctor wisely and well, but that, if known to many patients, would adversely affect the doctor-patient relationships.

Consider, for example, a doctor in a small town, married to the School Superintendent and also the mother of three children. In the eyes of this uptight little community, she is an utterly sober and proper young woman, also an excellent surgeon. They are unaware that she worked her way through medical school as a belly dancer, and she continues to enjoy belly-dancing as an important part of her self-expression.

Of course, a few of her patients might find it amusing and a human touch to know that once a year, when she is ostensibly visiting art museums in Europe, she is actually undulating under a pseudonym (and little else) at a London bistro. But for the majority, knowledge of such activities would utterly contradict their image of the kind of person who is a reliable doctor. Not only that, but it would be difficult for them to accept as their superintendent of schools a man with such a wife.

In reality, her annual escapade gives her a tremendous lift and actually helps her function better as a wife, mother, and doctor the rest of the year. But this is a reality which only a few would understand and accept. Therefore, she wisely limits her belly-dancing to her private sector.

In this particular case, if you are wondering, her husband definitely knows about her dancing and he helps her maintain her Compartment Four *vis-à-vis* the community.

The role of Compartment Four in the relationship between spouses is like the relationship between doctor and patients. It is a time when one does things that do not in fact threaten the spouse or the marriage, but which would rub against the biases of the spouse if they were known about; a time for independent decisions.

Having arbitrarily divided the life of a typical doctor into three compartments and then added a fourth, let us now do the same with regard to a marriage:

Compartment One: This is the time one spends with one's spouse. It includes direct person-to-person activities like sex, and also things like teaming-up in bridge or tennis games with friends. It includes discussing the family's finances. And surprising as it may seem, Compartment One can also include swinging. For after all, swinging is viewed by most of its married devotees as something to do together.

Compartment Two: This is time the partners spend apart from one another, but in activities that have to do rather directly with their relationship: home, family, and so forth. If there are children, it includes things done with, or for, the children. A perfect example of a Compartment Two activity is husband John going to the store to select a birthday present for his wife. He may keep the trip a secret temporarily, but eventually she will open the present. In less romantic terms, Compartment Two is the sector for grocery marketing, chauffeuring the children, house-cleaning, picking up theater tickets, taking the television set to be repaired, and other mundane activities.

Compartment Three: Whatever time the marriage partners are doing something that has no direct relationship to each other or the life they share is the third segment. This includes jobs, of course, and the wife's golf and business trips, the husband's garden club, or whatever else occurs. This time is accountable in principle. That is, in sexually monogamous marriages, Compartment Three does not include love affairs. In an open marriage, Compartment Three might also include affairs, if there are any.

Compartment Four: Free time for independent decisions and private activities, limited only by practical considerations and your own conscience. There is no abandonment of responsibility, but neither is there the need to get spouse approval. Of course your spouse's value system will be fed into your computerized decision, but the final decision is yours. It is most important that you feel good about these independent decisions; that your gut tells you it is right for you. There is always the outside chance that your spouse will somehow, some way, find out. If you can fantisize standing up to your spouse and earnestly stating that you did what you needed for yourself and tried to avoid hurting him or her . . . and mean it . . . you are on the right path. If on the other hand an unexpected discovery would make you feel guilty, make you feel like a child who had disobeyed a parent, or make you feel like a mean bastard beating up an innocent victim, the chances are you, yourself, really don't believe the activity is legitimate. If you truly believe your experience was legitimate for you, no one has the power to change that view. You cannot be responsible for how someone else responds to your value judgment. What too often happens is that we tend to be dishonest with ourselves to avoid confrontation.

Many persons allow someone else, spouse, children, boss, etc., to intimidate them, to cause them to doubt their independent value judgment, and often they become guilty and ashamed. It is essential that you believe firmly in your decisions. Compartment Four is a time for responsible decisions, not a license to cheat.

But, many readers will argue, what about breaking the marriage contract? Most married partners have committed themselves to sexual monogamy. Our answer is, that is true. And if your conscience prohibits you from breaking that contract, however young you were, however meager your alternative, then outside sex is not for you. Your Compartment Four can be used only for those activities that are morally acceptable to you. Our point is that it is *your* right, guided by *your* conscience, to make the decision, not your spouse's. When marriage is limited to three compartments, it is not acknowledged that either partner has a right to make independent decisions. Such an acknowldgement would threaten the illusion—or ideal—that the couple "should" form a unity with complete honesty between them about all major issues. However, as we have pointed out, the seeds of Compartment Four are already present in the generally accepted (though unvoiced) rule that one does not open the other's mail or listen in on phone conversations on the extension. Once the general principle of privacy is accepted, what remains is rationally to determine how far privacy might be extended with beneficial results.

How much free time is reasonable? It depends on the situation of the couple, and of course this differs widely. For those with small children and very little money for baby-sitters, it may be difficult for either spouse to have Compartment Four more than once or twice a

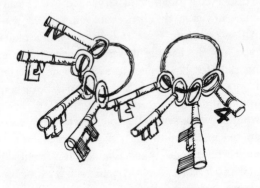

month. For those without children and with extra money, more free time and more different activities will be available.

Needless to say, Compartment Four will probably require that each spouse have a certain amount of "fun money" to spend without having to report back to the partner. Again, how much depends entirely on the circumstances. For the struggling young couple, Compartment Four money may be quite limited. For the well-to-do, $1,000 a year might never be missed. But the usefulness of Compartment Four is that the free time itself can be acknowledged although the specific activities are not shared. What you do on your own time is between you and your conscience and will not be reported back to the spouse, but he or she is quite aware that you have a private sector. For that reason, factors like time and money can ideally be discussed and negotiated in terms of realities.

Of course, it is quite possible that some irresponsible people will still supplement their Compartment Four money by unsavory methods —the children's piggy banks, the retirement fund at work the spouse doesn't know about, the $100 bill that Uncle Eli sent in the envelope addressed to both of you, and so on. The fact is that irresponsible people will tend to act irresponsibly, with or without a fourth compartment.

Ideally, Compartment Four is an agreed-upon part of the marriage understanding. Sometimes, however, it may be necessary for one spouse to unilaterally decide to introduce a private compartment into his or her own life. In that regard, we see two possibilities:

1.	You might tell the partner something like, "I have a private compartment in my life—I hope you do too, if you need it. I just need some private time when I don't have to be worried about what you might think. Even if I knew I was going to tell you about it later on, the whole idea of feeling obligated to report to you makes me feel like a child. I hope you'll understand. If not, what can I say? I love you very much."

Or:

2.	You might not tell your partner, and cover your fourth compartment time and activities in the traditionally clandestine ways. This is similar to what many people are doing now. But the inwardly felt stigma of cheating and deception is not a part of Compartment Four, even if it's unilateral. Instead, there is a clear, inward acceptance that you are fulfilling a need, demonstrating that you are a person and not part of an institution, that you are doing something for yourself rather than to someone, and that you have a perfect right to make independent decisions. You do not have to go through your spouse's conscience to decide what is right and best for you. This is not a privilege someone else has the power to grant—it is an inalienable right. Although mutual agreement is preferable, if it is not possible, take Compartment Four for yourself and proudly.

At this point, you may recognize that you have had a compartment without knowing it. What we are calling Compartment Four, you may have been calling "my night out" or "my separate vacation."

However, other readers may be asking the question raised earlier with regard to the doctor, that is, why should people want time to do things that they would not want to tell their spouses about? It may appear to some that Compartment Four is little more than a sophisticated way to have sexual affairs.

Our answer is that Compartment Four is far more inclusive than that, and might not include sex at all. There are many things people would like to do that have little or nothing to do with sex, yet their spouses strongly object to these activities. One of our requisites for a successful marriage is to allow your partner a little madness. As Zorba the Greek says, "Man needs a little madness to cut the chains and be free."

Remember that we all have our biases and prejudices. They are irrational and we can try to outgrow them, but as things stand now, they are ours, and we tend to defend them vigorously.

The problem is that when you form a pair–bond like marriage, you double your biases. Perhaps the increment is somewhat less than double. In any case, your behavior is now circumscribed not only by your own biases, but also by those of your spouse. If most of your biases and hang-ups are shared ones, you are fortunate. However, this is seldom the case, with the result that one spouse may look askance at things the other has done for years with great enjoyment and no pain of conscience. And even if the spouse has minimum biases, the way-out ideas that jump into your head may still wither and die, because they are counter to the "collective biases of society"—otherwise known as "cultural norms."

"Drat!" she said to herself, "here it is 4 A.M. and I have a craving for pickles and ice cream! But I'm not pregnant," she muses, "so how can I claim to want pickles and ice cream?"

Sometimes what is "madness" to your spouse is not so frivolous and still is thwarted by the limits of traditional marriage. These desires can appear quite acceptable to some people—but not to your spouse. And there's the rub. To illustrate this, we have composed a fictitious and admittedly whimsical little story:

Once upon a time, Rose lived on the other side of the tracks with her parents, seven siblings, and fourteen cats. Their yard was filled with broken beer bottles, and hot rods in various states of rust and disrepair. Rose's big brothers went to the stock car races every Saturday. Her big sisters loved indoor roller skating. When Rose was fourteen—and she was big for her age—she skated in her first Roller Derby. On television!

And Rose was the star. She pulled more hair, slugged more refs, and cursed louder than anybody. But how she could skate!

Then along came Jack. Jack didn't live on the other side of the tracks. He lived in the big house on top of the hill with his father, who was the president of the bank; his mother, who wore designer clothes, jewels and furs; and a pedigreed Dachshund. There were no rusting autos in their yard. It wasn't even a yard. It was called the grounds. And there were groundskeepers.

Then one day, Jack met Rose. "How old are you?" he said. "Fourteen," she answered. "My, you are big for your age," he thought. And so Jack eventually asked Rose to go steady. Now, Jack was really turned on by Rose. But he didn't like her manners. She called her derriere an "ass" and used "ain't" in the third person singular. He wanted to take her to the club, but how could he?

Jack decided to turn Rose into a lady.

First, he took her to La Parisienne and bought her two lovely gowns, a simple but very expensive pants suit, a gold charm bracelet, and three pairs of shoes. He also bought her beautiful lingerie and a very high-styled swim suit with matching coat.

"Now I could take her to the club," he thought. "But what about the way she talks?"

And so Jack worked with Rose on her speech. Fortunately, she was as bright as she was attractive. And in no time at all, she managed to sound like she came not from the hill, but from the clouds above it.

"Now I could take her to the club," he thought. "But what if she mentions roller derbies?"

"One last thing, Rose," he said. "Please don't utter a word about the derbies. As for myself, I've nothing against them. But would the people at the club understand? Hardly!"

And so Rose went to the club. All eyes were on her. And what bearing! What class! What a derriere!

Jack's mother called Rose "a fine young woman with the stuff to rise above her surroundings." Three years went by.

Then one day, Jack said, "Will you marry me?"

Rose grew dizzy. Her knees began to wobble. Visions of life on the hill flashed through her head.

"Wow!" she said. "Wow!"

"Just one last thing," Jack said. "Promise me, darling, never to skate again! The wife of Jackson V. Snodgrass is a lady from head to toe, seven days a week!"

"If that's the way you wish it, my darling, so be it," said Rose. "A lady from head to toe—seven days a week! That's me!"

And so, Jack and Rose were married and went to live on the hill. Rose loved their five acres. She learned all about gardening, and supervised the yard man tending the rose bushes. The children came—one, two, three—and of course a maid, too. And the name of Mrs. Jackson V. Snodgrass frequently appeared on the society pages. Rose liked everything about her new life!

But alas, one day, she came across the following in the morning paper:

> ROLLER SKATE? Good, experienced skaters needed for Smithville League, now in formation. Tryouts Thurs., Fri., 2–4 P.M., Smithville Roller-Rama, 918 S. Artesian.

Oh, how Rose was tempted. For two days, she resisted. "But I promised!" she thought to herself.

Thursday came, and there was a digging through old boxes in the attic in search of her skates. She walked over to the attic window and looked at them in the light. She spun the wheels with her fingers. She dreamed of fistfuls of hair, and took a swing at the villainous ref while the crowds roared. She skated faster and faster, around and around and around.

"But I can't," she thought.

Oh, ho, ho! You can't?

After lunch, Rose let it be known that she was going shopping. Under her arm, she carried a small, innocent brown paper bag. But inside that bag nothing was innocent. She carried a pair of roller skates!

Rose hopped into her Porsche and was on the way to Smithville.

The tryouts consisted of three events: hair pulling, ref slugging, and cussing. Rose won all three and was signed on by the Death Angels, the toughest team in town. Just to be sure, they asked her to skate once around the rink before they let her go home.

Rose felt guilty. Rose felt awful! Here she was, all signed up, but how could she ever get out of the house? On Tuesday nights?

Fortunately, Rose belonged to a sophisticated book club, and that very week a book about independent decisions in marriage arrived. She looked at the chapters and wondered what Compartment Four was all about. Because she had gone to rapid reading classes, Rose finished it in thirty-five minutes. She was breathless, exhilarated, wild with excitement.

"I need a Compartment Four!" she said to herself.

And then she shouted to the four grass-papered walls, "I need a Compartment Four!"

Just then, Jack walked in.

"For God's sake! What's this Compartment Four that you need?" he asked. "We have fourteen rooms and five baths already!" With her chin up and fire in her eyes, she said, "Darling, I've something to tell you. Something very important! I deserve to have a private compartment in our marriage. I am not speaking of cheating and deception. Rather, I have just arrived at a clear inward acceptance that this is an inalienable right!"

"A private compartment?" Jack said.

"Tuesday nights?" Rose said.

"If it's for roller skating, don't say so!" Jack said.

"I won't." Rose said.

"Nobody will ever know?" Jack said. "After all, I am vice-president now."

"Nobody will ever know," Rose said. "Not even you, darling, I promise. You've trusted me all these years. Trust me now!"

And so if ever you visit the Smithville Roller-Rama of a Tuesday evening, you will see Rose there. But we won't tell you what she looks like. She's disguised, we'll say that much. But Compartment Four is hers. We wish her luck!

The above story was intended to provide a light touch, but its point is an earnest one: *Compartment Four provides opportunities for role-free behavior.* Rose's roller skating might not be well-regarded by her husband and his socialite friends. But it is important to her, and Compartment Four is her time for it.

Compartment Four is a vacation from roles.

But we are not suggesting that roles be done away with. Roles are essential to all societies. We would be in sad shape if the doctor said, "Gee, I don't think I feel like being a doctor today—I feel more like fishing. Maybe if I feel like being a doctor tomorrow, I'll do a little surgery."

Not only are roles necessary for society to function, but they are important to one's psychological well-being. In that regard, many people past retirement age are role-deprived. They are deprived of the social and occupational roles that help to structure time and provide a feeling that one is a productive and needed member of society. In this age of the nuclear family, even the role of grandparent is relatively superficial. Most elderly people need to be provided with more roles. To have roles

is, in essence, to be recognized as a member of society. And this is true of all societies.

At the same time, however, our particular culture is overly concerned with roles. When you ask someone, "What are you?" the expected reply is "I'm a machinist" (or a lawyer, or a housewife, and so forth). But each of us is much more than our occupational role. We are more even than the sum total of all the various roles we play in a lifetime. To be fully human is to play roles and also to break free of them and transcend them. There are times when persons need to break free of and transcend even the role of spouse. In that regard, role and image are similar. We would define role as the way one behaves and/or is expected to behave in a particular situation: mother with sick child, doctor with patient, boss with employee, and so on. We would define image as the kind of person other people need, or want, to think you are. In terms of image, Rose's husband might feel, "How could a man in my position have as a wife a woman who skates in roller derbies?" However, since her image is protected by Compartment Four, he can happily make love to her several times a week.

In our earlier example of the belly-dancing doctor, many people in the small town would feel, "I couldn't trust a doctor who belly-dances." However, since she does it in London under a pseudonym while ostensibly on a grand tour, her professional image is safeguarded.

A woman who despises gay people may be happily married to a virile bisexual man who makes love to her six nights a week, the exception being Thursday night when he drinks beer with the boys. She simply does not know that the boys are gay.

In all three of these examples, the private compartment of life allows people to express facets of their personalities that are vital to them, and to do so without disrupting the feelings and lives of others.

Some moralists and marriage counselors suggest that when you really love someone, you should love the whole person and everything about them. This would imply, in our view, doing away with the roles and images that are typical of most marriages. But how many mothers usually feel like changing diapers, helping with homework, holding bloody noses, or mending doll clothes? We believe that fathers could learn to share more of these tasks. These days, happily, many are! How many really feel like caring for a seriously ill spouse for month after month? To be oneself implies either not doing it, or groaning and mumbling, so that the ill person feels even worse. To ask that you love *everything* about your favorite people or that you like doing *everything* you do for them is an irrational request.

That being the case, we feel that vacations from daily routines and also from favorite people are needed by almost everyone. Even Jesus, who is celebrated for his ability to accept the outcast lepers and dregs of society, withdrew into the wilderness for forty days and forty nights to consult his God and his conscience. In another instance, he withdrew to the mountaintop to escape from the crowds of people. Most of us need our mountaintops. These days, however, the only retreat many of us have, hounded as we are by kids, dogs, neighbors, and spouses, is to go into the bathroom and lock it. Many read, meditate, think, or simply luxuriate in a tub of warm water, utterly undisturbed. The bathroom has become the final sanctuary. And this is absurd—each of us deserves privacy beyond the limits of a tiled, locked cubicle crowded with the accouterments of plumbing.

Many people no longer in the height of in-loveness are desperate for the kind of freedom afforded by Compartment Four. Of course, the need for variety and the need to get away vary greatly. Some persons whose lives and marriages are relatively dull and whose spouses are nice but not very imaginative need time to hang loose. Others, with hectic households of never a dull moment and practical jokers for mates, would find the cemetery a welcome relief.

Compartment Four marriages, like most human relationships, will continue to have their roles and images. But liberated partners recognize that if there are no vacations from role-playing, the performance tends to go stale and lose its zip. They do not place odious limitations on each other's personal freedom or engage in truth sessions that can be equally odious and emotionally damaging. Their marriages emphasize mutual respect between separate individuals, each of whom has an inalienable right to a certain amount of autonomy and independence.

The principle of Compartment Four is:

I respect myself—including my own peculiar needs or desires. I also respect my partner. Therefore, if I know through experience that some decisions and activities that are vitally important to me would be upsetting to my spouse, Compartment Four allows me to separate the two. Compartment Four actualizes my right to autonomy and privacy as an individual. It provides a temporary freedom from the role of spouse. It is accountable only to my own conscience. There is no show and tell. And there are no strings attached.

Rather than working out point-by-point agreements about which kinds of behavior are allowable and which aren't, it is much more rational simply to agree that each partner deserves some independence and a reasonable amount of free time. A continuous asking of permission to do thus-and-such is demeaning and implies that one's marriage partner is one's warden, a rather disturbing implication, to say the least. This is quite readily bypassed by Compartment Four.

And at the same time, neither spouse must endure the rubbing of salt into his or her wounds, which is what often happens in traditional marriage when one of them strays from tradition and then feels a need to confess to the other. Such confessions may seem good for the soul, but they are not always good for the partner or the marriage.

Consider, for example, the difficulty one may encounter in getting spousal agreement to a specific behavior:

W: Well, how did you like it?
H: Best beef stroganoff I ever had!
W: No, Honey, not the dinner—the book!
H: Book?
W: Didn't you finish it yet?
H: What book?
W: The book about liberated marriage and Compartment Four.
H: Oh, that. I just glanced through it.
W: Well, did you like it?
H: What part?
W: Dating after marriage. Now there's something I wish I'd thought of!
H: I can see that some people might like it.
W: And it wouldn't hurt their marriage, right?
H: Why should it? They both agree. It's all open and above board.
W: But of course, you have to be nonpossessive. That's the best way to be, don't you think so?
H: Be what?
W: Nonpossessive—not jealous!
H: Of course. Why be jealous? What a waste of good emotion. If they want to have dates, more power to them. After all, these are modern times. Things aren't like they used to be.
W: I'm glad you agree.
H: Of course I agree! I think it's great, these young people with their new ideas. It's like a breath of fresh air. I hope everybody reads it. That's what we need—new ideas! I think people would be a lot better off.
W: Oh, Honey, by the way. . . .
H: I can hear it coming. Okay, the eaves troughs. For the thousandth time, I'll clean them. Sunday.

W: No, not that.

H: What, then?

W: I'm glad you agree.

H: Agree?

W: Didn't you agree that dating after marriage is a good idea?

H: Of course I agree. How many times do I have to tell you? I agree! In fact, I'll go further than that.

W: You will?!

H: I certainly will. I think Mike and Gretta should read it. I think that's just what they need.

W: Honey?

H: Huh?

W: Uh . . . I'm glad you agree because, uh, well, I kind of, well, have a, I guess you'd call it a date! There, I've said it! I've come right out and said it!

H: The hell, you say! With whom?

W: See, Mike and Gretta have already read the book and. . . .

H: You're going out with that Mike? Like hell you are! Why I wouldn't trust that (expletive deleted) as far as I could throw that (expletive deleted) book!

W: But I thought you already agreed!

H: Sure, you bet, I agreed all right—but I sure didn't agree about you! Not on your life!

W: Then you're an exclusive-possessivist pig!

H: Who said anything about being a . . . what was that you called me?

W: I said you're jealous! You're exclusive!

H: I am not jealous. Who said anything about being jealous? I just said you're not going out with that (expletive deleted) Mike Steinholder!

W: Then you don't trust me! How can you be married to somebody you don't even trust?

H: Of course I trust you.

Perhaps this particular lady would have encountered less difficulty had she gone after an agreement that she deserved some free time, rather than seeking agreement to specifically date a neighbor.

Some couples, however, do agree to specific kinds of extramarital behavior such as dating, and even include an overly exuberant, "Have fun!" as the spouse goes out the door. This may be followed by a panicstricken dash to the dresser drawer to count the condoms or make sure the foam is still there. The pill and sterilization tend to modify that scene. Still, the dating spouse may come home at one o'clock to find John or Jill pacing the floor, the Scotch bottle half empty, the ashtray full.

W: Sorry I'm late. What kept you up?

H: Oh, I don't know. Just restless, I guess.

W: Gosh, I hope you weren't worried about me!

H: Oh, no, of course not.

W: Well, I could understand if you were. But really, everything's cool. Please don't worry.

H: I didn't think your going out would get me uptight—but I guess it does.

W: I'm the same way.

H: The same way?

W: When you go out.

H: Kind of uptight and apprehensive?

W: Kind of. But I pretend to be asleep when you come home, so you won't worry, you know, about my being worried!

H: You know what?

W: What?

H: I'm glad you're home, and I love you!

W: I love you, too, better than soup and sandwiches! Hey, you're not chickening out, are you?

H: On what?

W: On our each going out sometimes with other people.

H: Not if you're not.

W: I'm not. I mean we haven't tried it much yet.

H: Me either. Let's try it another month and see if things are still okay.

W: Know what?

H: What?

W: I want you right now! How's that for reassurance?
H: Great! Let's go!

This outcome is ideal. Each openly admits that the other's dating causes anxiety. But they are able to reassure each other of the concern and love they feel without chickening out on a course of action they had carefully thought about and which they agreed would be best for their relationship, at least for the time being. However, the outcome will not always be so ideal, and with other individuals, the above scene could have turned into a blow-up:

W: Sorry I'm so late. What kept you up?
H: Oh, I don't know. Just restless, I guess.
W: Gosh, I hope you weren't worried about me!
H: Oh, no, of course not.
W: Well, don't you want to know if I had fun?
H: Yes, did you?
W: Don't be so damned nosy. You knew I had a date.
H: Sorry I asked.
W: Sorry? Who said you should be sorry?
H: Because you don't want to tell me.
W: Tell you what?
H: If you had a good time.
W: Why should I tell you. Listen, don't you trust me?
H: Of course I trust you.
W: Well then can't I have a good time without telling you I had a good time?
H: Hey, just what kind of a good time did you have, anyway?
W: Wouldn't you like to know!
H: Screw you!

It would have been less risky for this couple to agree on Compartment Four without agreeing to dating specifically—though in this instance, we wonder if even that would have been possible! This couple's intellectual ideal—that they should be able to date—exceeds their emotional grasp and their ability to handle it graciously.

But as a rule, the fact that Compartment Four is a "Private–Keep Out" personal sanctuary eliminates the need for the grotesque deceptions and alibis that traditionally accompany clandestine affairs. With Compartment Four, the existence of "my own free time to make my own free decisions" is at least acknowledged unless, of necessity, it must be unilateral.

We feel that Compartment Four is especially necessary in marriages where one spouse is unusually possessive and restrictive so that the other has to run a mine field just to do things that most of us take for granted. We know of a husband caught in that trap, a charming man who feels loyalty to the marriage vows, adores his one son, and would never leave his wife. But oh, how he would like a little freedom!

His wife does not drink at all and she is unwilling to have his friends stop in on the spur of the moment for a beer, or even a coke. "If you insist on having guests, give me a few days' lead time so the house will be ready," she says. "And please—no beer! You know how I hate the smell!" At the same time, she is unwilling for him to stay after work for a beer with the boys. Whenever he wants to stop for a beer, he has to have an airtight alibi about a business appointment and then gargle three times on the way home.

So this man's wife is too rigid, and he has the satisfaction of knowing that most marriage counselors would agree. But of what value is it to him to understand that his wife is unusually strict? It doesn't change things. However, if the climate of opinion changed so that people anticipated and accepted time off as a routine part of the marriage understanding, one spouse's hang-ups wouldn't either hog tie the other or force this absurd hypocrisy.

Even in a fairly good marriage, it is sometimes difficult to ask to go out on your own. It can easily be misinterpreted as a form of rejection. Consider an Italian girl married to a Swede. She is a girl who likes to go back to her old neighborhood to eat her favorite pasta and speak Italian with her friends and relatives. She has a good marriage, but it's awkward for her to go to the old neighborhood because her husband feels that maybe he should accompany her. When she says no, he begins to wonder if something is going on so that perhaps she doesn't want him along. Granted that this might be cleared up by better communications, isn't it much easier just to accept the broad principle of freedom and privacy, the basic right of every marriage partner to some autonomy?

In summary, to start listing all the behavior patterns that should or should not be acceptable is demeaning and impractical. It is both more dignified and more functional to include time without strings attached. It is more respectful to allow each actor to make an independent judgment than for one spouse to pass judgment on the other. Therefore, we believe that a single, straightforward agreement to have time off from marriage is far better than having to ask continuously for permission to do other things. In fact, we do not believe that either spouse has the right, capacity, or authority to grant permission to the other to do or not do anything that does not directly relate to themselves. Granting permission reflects parent/child, teacher/pupil interaction, not an adult transaction.

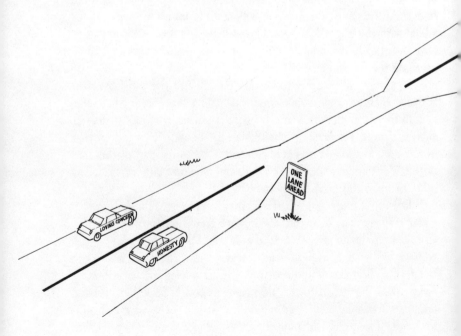

Of course, the point will be raised that not everyone will use Compartment Four responsibly. We admit that possibility. And no rules we might suggest will turn irresponsible people into paragons. Nevertheless, we would like to introduce a single rule. It is this:

No great big chickens are to come home to roost. Little chickens may be unavoidable. But please, no great big ones! For example:

W: Isn't life great since we've each had our Compartment Four?
H: Yes, except, I hate to tell you, dear, but I've been spending my Compartment Four at the racetracks and, well, we'll have to sell the house.
W: Oh, no! It must be the syphilis you caught from me! It must have affected your brain.
H: Syphilis? What are you talking about?
W: I didn't want to tell you, darling, because I caught it on my Compartment Four time. But you know that chancre on your lip that went away?
H: Oh, no!

These are great big chickens. Compartment Four does not give one diplomatic immunity from the consequences of one's actions! Assuming the absence of big chickens, Compartment Four is unaccountable time.

In case the reader does not yet fully understand, here is an additional litany of the virtues of Compartment Four: It reminds each spouse of the privacy and independence of the other. And it reminds each spouse of his or her own privacy and independence. Compartment Four is designed to respect differences rather than to put down the partner. Compartment Four helps to maintain some of that sense of mystery that is intriguing. We believe that romance is fed by a certain amount of mystery and that too much familiarity can breed boredom, if not genuine contempt.

Compartment Four substitutes conscience for mere fear of disapproval by the spouse. In the language of transactional analysis, it puts the adult in charge, not the child.

It also encourages each partner to explore and do things on his own. In that regard, it is good medicine for overly-dependent people.

Compartment Four makes it hard to go on playing the game, "If it weren't for him (her), I'd. . . ." Since the spouse's approval is no longer at issue, the hang-ups that prevent one from reaching for life are now experienced as one's own. And that can be damned uncomfortable!

So you're convinced. You've discussed Compartment Four with your partner, if that is possible in your marriage, and you each agree that it's a good idea.

And now it's Thursday night—your first night off. You may be one of those people who take to a private compartment like a duck takes to water. But on the other hand, for those with small children and crowded schedules, it may be somewhat unnerving to be suddenly confronted with four hours of unaccountable free time. Looking forward to freedom is one thing. Using it creatively and responsibly is something else. It is a well-known fact that some ex-convicts, finally out on parole, commit crimes in order to get sent back to prison. In the same way, one can be institutionalized by marriage. Once that is allowed to happen, Compartment Four can be scary.

Thus, one's first Compartment Four evening might include thoughts like:

"Wow! Here I am! Compartment Four time! Now, let's see. What shall I do? Oh, boy! A whole four hours! How about a flick? (Reads the entertainment section in the paper.) Nothing good on. Let's see. I know! A bar! Delaney's? Haven't been there in years. But the old gang wouldn't be there. Wouldn't know anybody. Well, let's see. (Walking along Clark Street.) There's that poster on the Gestalt Theater. (Looks at watch.) I've still got time to get there. But wait a minute. What's that it says? Audience participation? Sounds kind of scary to me. To hell with that stuff, baby. Oh well, the library then. Oh. It closes at nine. What'll I do after that? I said I'd be out till twelve. After all this hassle to get free time, I'd feel like a dog with its tail between its legs coming home early. Darn it! I wish my husband (wife) were here! He (she) can always think of something to do!"

This will not be everyone's experience. But if this is how your private compartment starts out, don't give up. Keep at it! Plan your next Compartment Four ahead of time. It's a healthy challenge, in our view, to be forced to structure one's own time once in a while, and a great opportunity to discover, or rediscover, what you yourself like to do. And in that regard, Compartment Four can produce growth experiences.

For individuals who find it very difficult to plan and do something on their own, we are not being facetious in suggesting that the time be spent in a personal growth group or T-group led by a competent professional.

In other words, the problem will not always be time. Many middle-aged housewives have loads of free time, time filled with knitting, housekeeping, and other stereotypical activities. The problem is not getting out physically, but getting out psychologically. It is possible intellectually to include the idea of a private sector in your philosophy of marriage, but still feel like a prisoner. Things one dreamed of doing all these years may suddenly seem scary. One may feel like the small boy observed running round and round the block. "What are you doing?" asked a passerby. "I'm running away from home," he answered. "Oh?" "Well, I *am!* But my mother said I mustn't cross the street!"

Erich Fromm's book *Escape from Freedom* discussed many of the ways in which people seek to avoid responsibility for personal choice. In the same way, one might seek to avoid the wide range of choices opened up by private free time. If so, the experience may bring home how much one has been leaning on a spouse, and on the marriage role for identity, direction, and structuring of activities, using the marriage to escape from freedom. The same can be true of other kinds of live-in arrangements, be they straight or gay.

Just the opposite of escaping from freedom, Compartment Four is a marital Magna Carta of personal liberty. Of course, it is not complete liberty all the time. One continues to function as a responsible spouse, parent, and so forth. But now, there is an added private compartment. We advocate Compartment Four not to subvert marriage, but to clarify the right to some freedom and privacy for each partner.

Like all kinds of liberty, the private sector requires a kind of vigilance to keep it from slipping away. For that reason, we recommend that Compartment Four time, once established, be used regularly. "Gotta use it or you'll lose it!" It may suffice to follow the pattern of someone we know. If two weeks go by and he hasn't scheduled anything exciting for his weekly time off, he acts just as if he had. He dresses up, says, "See

you about twelve, Honey" as he goes out the door, drives to a nearby cafe, and catches up on his reading, over coffee. He arrives home promptly at midnight. Because he happens to use Compartment Four for occasional outside sex, he doesn't want to attract any undue attention, as would be the case if six months went by and then suddenly he started going out often.

We have referred to the private sector as a right. Without compromising that position, we also find it helpful to think of it as a privilege. That is, even though one has a right to privacy, the spouse's anger would be justified if big chickens came home to roost consistently, or if one said, "I'm going out for my Compartment Four evening," and disappeared for a week. With regard to Compartment Four, we feel it is especially important to be home when you say you'll be home! It is important to build up one another's confidence that the private compartment does not undermine other commitments.

When Compartment Four is new to a couple, there may be twinges of possessive jealousy. However, the chances are that dealing with these feelings will be a healthy growth experience. Some people handle the jealousy problem by going out on the same evening. If there are children, a sitter is hired. Each partner is so busy doing his or her own thing that there is little time for morbid preoccupation about the other's activities.

Finally, we admit, there are partners who simply will not agree to the idea of a private compartment, or who will feel no need for it in their lives. It may seem too threatening, or seem unnecessary in the context of a superb relationship.

At the opposite extreme will be those who are married in name only, so independent that no further encouragement is needed. Their whole life is a private compartment. We also realize that in our highly mobile society, many partners already have had too many days off for the good of the relationship. Spouses whose work frequently takes them out of town are the most striking examples. And though many in that category have strings attached, the strings are mere threads when compared to those of the nine-to-five worker who can never leave town. Those whose lives already have too much Compartment Four may be in need of compartments One, Two, and Three described earlier. Still, we believe that the philosophy of this book may be helpful, both in creating a healthy attitude toward time away and in promoting the same kind of freedom for the spouse who is often left at home.

In the same regard, we recognize that many spouses, especially women, do not want the kind of freedom implied by Compartment Four. Already they don't see enough of their husbands. They want more married nights, not fewer. Our answer is that Compartment Four is an option for those who choose it, not a requirement.

The authors feel that a sense of aliveness is, in part, the product of vital interplay between the kinds of experiences listed, for contrast, in these two columns:

Sharing	Privacy
Known	Unknown

Interdependent	Independent
Safe Harbor	Open Sea
Commitment	No Strings Attached
Safety	Risk
Role-fulfilling	Role-free
Team Effort	Individual Effort
Expectations	Surprises

We do not say that the column on the left is necessarily a description of marriage, or that the righthand column applies to Compartment Four, because ingenious couples are able to bring many role-free, surpriseful elements into their marriages. In that regard, it is clear that couples, as couples, need time to do things together that are temporarily exploratory, adventuresome, playful—to "do it in the backyard," if you will! Couples need time to be only with each other, free of the expectations of children, parents, the community, and employers.

And at the same time, we know people whose clandestine affairs and/or Compartment Four activities are familiar, safe, dependable, and even role-fulfilling. For example, a woman whom we interviewed has maintained a single clandestine affair for more than twenty years with a quiet guy who has few surprises to offer. Each time they meet, they go through the same routines. The affair is a harbor for both of them, involves little risk or growth, and is definitely role-structured both sexually and otherwise.

But for a majority, marriage is mostly the column on the left, comfortable and uncomfortable routines. To the degree that life is lacking, what is lacking is on the right: the chance to step out of one's usual roles, to take interpersonal risks that can lead to growth, to venture into new relationships and experiences. For those whose lives otherwise lack many such experiences, Compartment Four provides excellent opportunities. Rather, Compartment Four doesn't provide them, it is no magic process—you do! Calling it Compartment Four makes it easier.

We hesitated to list work on the left and play on the right. However, a useful analogy might be drawn from the tension between them. Most analyses we have read affirm that even in the smooth marriages celebrated in popular magazines, the partners are in fact working to keep the marriage alive and exciting. Such work is similar to the work of a doctor devoted to his practice. In both, there is a great deal of emotional involvement, effort, and satisfaction. But rarely does the doctor feel he doesn't need a vacation, despite his love for his work.

Needing vacations and days off from marriage, or any other close pair-bond, does not mean one does not love one's partner. In fact, if it weren't for imposed separations, the need of most couples for vacations from each other would be obvious. We conceded that there would be exceptions, just like the old family doctor who never took a vacation in his life.

If we accept the concept that a good marriage demands work and the partners deserve a vacation, then how much more needed is a vacation for those working at less satisfactory marriages! For some people, marriage and the home are little more rewarding than an assembly-line job, distinctly lacking peaks of emotional satisfaction. Persons in such marriages often stay married for reasons not unlike those of the workers who punch in each day, who know which side their bread is buttered on. By buttered, we mean not just finances, but the home, circle of friends, and the routines of years. In our view, this can be a perfectly sound, rational, healthy reason for staying married! But why not be honest and admit the need for vacations from such marriages?

To put it another way, many whose marriages consist mostly of routine, safety, and team efforts could use the private compartment for role-free behavior and independent efforts. Days off should allow for the opportunity to lose one's identity, if the need is there. The lawyer who plays golf or goes fishing is certainly vacationing, but remains always the lawyer. But the lawyers who race stock cars, play drums, or belly-dance—these lawyers truly lose their identity on their time off. A wife or husband should be able to do the same in Compartment Four—unusual things that appeal to them, with their own conscience as guides, not "I can't, what would my partner say?"

We are not referring here to psychopathic activities and urges; these present special problems for which we have no easy answers.

We are thinking of nonpathological desires—to spend a week at the Zen Buddhist monastery (some spouses would object), to seek occasional sexual variety, and many other activities. Not all Compartment Four activities need be fun. If one's partner is a socialite, privacy might be needed to visit a relative in prison. There is a touching story of a young girl whose family demanded that she get rid of her dog. She told them she had given it away, but she made a home for the dog in an abandoned building. Each day after school, she visited her dog and brought it food.

When the private compartment is utilized to express usually hidden desires, it is not necessary to report details to the spouse. Some would not report drum-playing or belly-dancing. Others would hold back only on secrets relating to intimacy, romance, and sex. But rarely would anyone report *everything,* and never would one be required to report anything, if the principle of privacy is fully established.

History has always been filled with men who exercised this kind of freedom. But such marriages were always one-sided, with the wife forced to take it whether she liked it or not. Unfortunately, it appears that as women spoke out and demanded equality, the result was merely to curb husbands' freedoms to match wives' limitations, rather than to expand wives' freedoms to more nearly equal their husbands'. But if marriage is to remain a viable institution, we feel that the trend must be reversed in the direction of more freedom for both spouses. Sophisticated and liberated women simply will not fill the the traditional wife role. Nevertheless, many will marry, placing additional stress on the traditional marriage pattern. Others will avoid marriage, knowing that they can enjoy a career with decent income, a love partner, a home, a difficult but tolerable place in society, and opportunities for travel and close, warm relationships with other people's children. Some single women will *have* children.

Thus, for liberated women there must also be some form of liberated marriage or increasingly there will be no marriage at all for them. If so, we fear that the best potential mothers may be out of the marriage market. Then, perhaps, motherhood and marriage would be limited to those women who are willing to accept subservience, to be, in the words of Germaine Greer, "female eunuchs."

Often we are asked about the children. How will they fare if both parents demonstrate so much independence, both in terms of time away from home and emotional involvement outside the family? Our answer is that, assuming a minimum, the *quality* of time spent with children is far more important than the quantity. The emotional atmosphere that pervades the home—warmth, openness, hospitality, lack of tension and jealousy—is more important than how the atmosphere was created. If children had their druthers, we suspect thay would prefer a fun-loving mother at home only part time to a meticulously dutiful mother at home all the time.

Finally, how does the private compartment compare with various other strategies? Although our proposal of Compartment Four may not sound very radical to some, and altogether too radical to others, we feel that it introduces an element of individuality and freedom that certain other proposals lack.

For instance, Robert Rimmer in *Proposition 31* describes a group marriage where there is mutual love between previously-separate couples. They develop from good friends and neighbors through a stage of affairs and fears into a multiple marriage arrangement with free exchange of spouses. However, this new mode of living has its own strict rules. They exclude the possibility of sex outside the group. They agree that there will be no observers or additional participants. And so on. In other words, they expand the periphery of marriage privileges. But they do not make marriage a gravitational center, as we do, with each partner gaining new rights to personal freedom.

In addition, group marriage does not deal adequately with certain practical considerations of our highly mobile society. Imagine four or more adults, each with a different profession, trying to be fair when one of them is offered a great job opportunity in another city! Compartment Four marriage, of course, does not answer the problem either. But, at least, it is somewhat easier to solve when just two people are vitally affected by the decision.

Another pattern is the phenomenon known as swinging, to which we have alluded a number of times. This too is circumscribed by rules and boundaries. Swinging does not promote individual decision-making beyond the initial decision to join the Swingers Group. Even that may be a coercive decision, where the more forceful partner wants to swing but the other does not. Most swingers are proud of their rules. Rules lend an atmosphere of morality. Middle-class people are skilled in their ability to use strong language to describe what is *not* permitted in order to make what *is* permitted seem good and acceptable! "We don't allow homosexuals, therefore we are good. We don't allow single people, therefore we are good. We don't allow dating in-between parties, and so on." This approach takes extramarital sex, which in any other context most swinging couples would view as adultery, an avowed evil, and wraps it in a package acceptable to them. But adultery for a highly-sexed spouse with a sexually turned-off mate remains immoral.

In contrast, it is our sincere hope that we are projecting our ideas as guidelines rather than rules, that a private compartment is seen as an option, not a regulation. We are merely suggesting the responsible use of individual judgment and some ways to make that possible without rattling your partner's cage.

Another approach is suggested by Dr. George Bach in *The Intimate Enemy*. He suggests that many marital problems are often best handled by teaching couples how to deal with their conflicts openly. His approach, fight-training, is based on helping partners be more honest about their thoughts and especially about their feelings. His methods are aimed at the productive resolution of conflicts and, in that regard, we feel that he offers many excellent suggestions.

However, fight-training also has its limitations, as is true of all techniques. It cannot work for the couple where one is far better at fighting than the other, because defeat seems so inevitable to the poor fighter that he or she refuses to fight. In addition, we would point out that couples who come together for help have already taken the first big step—both members of the team have agreed that there is a problem and there is hope for a solution, or at least an improvement. But all too often, only one partner seeks help, the other believing that there is no problem or that there can be no improvement. Therefore, we are attempting to add other constructive ideas about marriage, a basic pattern that allows for each partner to develop more freely on his or her own.

Compartment Four may or may not directly improve the marriage or the relationships of those who live together without marriage. But it does offer opportunities for individual growth. It stands in contrast to traditional marriage, which offers only one size suit and asks all couples regardless of height, weight, or shape to fit into it.

We believe marriage can be made a more attractive option for

those who value personal freedom and the satisfactions and security of marriage or other committed relationships. These may never be wholly compatible, but a private compartment in marriage makes them more so.

chapter 5

the Limits of
open marriage

When Betty and Bob were first married, they pledged to be truly intimate all their lives. And so it was for the first several years. They began with the sparkles and excitement of mutual discovery. Then the baby arrived and, for them, this was an experience that brought them even closer together.

At the same time, Betty and Bob never intended to be possessive of each other. Each, they agreed, could have outside interests. In that regard, although Nena and George O'Neill had not yet written their book *Open Marriage*, Betty and Bob clearly enjoyed what the O'Neills would call an open contract. And so Betty would cheerfully kiss Bob goodbye when he left for his Chinese cooking class and warmly welcome him back. Bob would stay home with the baby while Betty attended the Chess Club meeting. And, more often than not, they made love when she came home.

But while each was free to enjoy outside activities, they also agreed that the "real thing" was to be only between themselves. And they seemed to have so much going for them during those early years that each looked askance at the idea of ever needing an affair. After all, how much emotional giving and receiving could one person enjoy or afford?

As the years went by, Bob and Betty continued to enjoy each other both sexually and in other ways. From time to time, they would introduce new twists into their sexual routine which they had read about or thought up on their own. A weekend workshop on human sexuality further expanded their freedom to enjoy each other. Perhaps they were not as deeply in love as in the early years, but their marriage was clearly neither dull nor unrewarding. Whatever other joys life might bring, Bob and Betty very much wanted their marriage to continue into the years ahead.

Thus, there was no unhappiness to drive either of them into an affair. But the warmth and security of their basically good marriage gave both Betty and Bob a surplus of warmth and energy that tended to spill over into outside activities and friendships. And although they had long ago agreed that the marriage would be the most important relationship in their lives, without having to be exclusive, Betty had never actively considered an affair.

Then, on a warm spring night just before the primaries, Betty attended a political rally. The speaker excited her. She felt herself becoming more and more turned on as he gave clear, forceful answers to the problems their community faced. She spoke to him afterwards, then went along with a small group of party leaders for coffee. The speaker, Cal, who was a candidate for a state office, was part of the group.

For Betty, it was an all–electric meeting. As they talked over coffee, she felt herself melting. When the group broke up, Cal escorted Betty to her car. "I'm going to be in town through tomorrow afternoon," he said. "How about meeting me for lunch?"

A year ago, or certainly five years ago, Betty's refusal would have come easily. Now, she found herself unable to say yes or no. On the one hand, she wanted to meet Cal for lunch and more! But she was afraid of the risks even as she yearned for new challenge and excitement. What an offer from *him*, of all people! But, she asked herself, don't affairs usually end up wrecking marriages? Or cause guilt feelings you can't handle?

Torn between doubt and desire, she begged off and drove home half fearing but half hoping he would call. What would she say if he did? Betty didn't know. It was clear, however, that she needed to take a fresh, in-depth look at her marriage and her own feelings about sex, love, personal growth, and extramarital relationships.

The next morning, Betty's head was full of nothing but Cal and her confusion about what to do. She called a friend with whom she could discuss personal problems in confidence. She told her friend about meeting Cal, his proposition, and the warmth and excitement she was feeling even now as she talked about him.

"I think I could handle an affair," Betty said, "but my worry is how to handle it with Bob. I'm capable of being cool and clandestine about it and he'd never know. But on the other hand, we've always been so straight and honest with each other! I mean, we've been able to share just about everything, even my silly fantasies and my ideas about being strong and independent and all that. And Bob has been able to tell me about his weaknesses, his wanting to cry sometimes, I don't think that's unmasculine. We've been so much on the level with each other for nine years I just hate to start lying now. But can I even tell him about last night? I mean, not just that I heard an exciting speaker, I already told him that, but about the gut responses, the butterflies, the proposition, and how much I want to say yes?"

"Have you read *Open Marriage* by Nena and George O'Neill?" her friend asked. "No? I'll bring it over then. It's super, and you've simply got to read it!"

Open Marriage, Betty discovered, described the very freedom to engage in a wide range of outside activities that she and Bob had enjoyed throughout their marriage. Open marriage is described by the O'Neills as an honest and open relationship between two people, based on the equal freedom and identity of both partners. It includes a commitment to the individual growth of each partner through an "openness to one's self, an openness to another's self, and an openness to the world."

Open Marriage does not emphasize extramarital sex, although the O'Neills do state that outside sexual experiences when they are in the context of a meaningful relationship may be rewarding and beneficial to an open marriage. Open marriage stresses honesty between marriage partners, yet, in the words of the O'Neills, "there is no place for what might be called vicious truths in marriage or in any good relationship." In fact, they emphasize, building toward greater honesty, and thus toward increased trust, must be carried out at a slow pace and with great caution in those marriages in which trust least exists. Spouses must be protective of each other's sensitive areas, and there is no excuse for disguising cruelty as honesty. "The object," say the O'Neills, "is to work toward greater honesty with consideration and judgment."

Betty had finished reading *Open Marriage* by mid-afternoon. "Well, now, do I tell Bob everything?" she asked herself. She and Bob clearly had an open marriage in every area up to, but not yet including, outside intimacies. Would this be one of those sensitive areas, for Bob, which she should protect? She decided to take the indirect approach—to first invite Bob to read the book and then discuss its ideas with him on a nonspecific level. She was especially eager to hear Bob's reactions to Chapter 16, in which the O'Neills discuss love and sex without jealousy. If he seemed to be overly anxious or suspicious talking about sexual affairs in the abstract, or about the possibility of honesty between them on that subject, she'd just back off and make her own separate decision about Cal. If, on the other hand, Bob seemed eager and ready for more openness, then she'd take the risk of sharing at least some of her gut responses about Cal.

The timing was perfect. In a few days, Bob had finished *Open Marriage* and was eager to talk. As it turned out, it was Bob who had most wanted to bring up this whole area, but he hadn't known how to begin. The book provided the perfect opportunity.

So for several evenings, Bob and Betty discussed their own relationship, and the idea of affairs, and how much honesty each felt he or she could live comfortably with. Both admitted that, while they loved one another and didn't want to do anything to hurt the marriage, there might come a time in the future when an affair might look appealing. They were still talking about the possibility of outside sex, not the reality.

But finally, Bob had enough of ideas and out came his confession. "I know outside sex wouldn't hurt our marriage," he said. "I've already done it and it hasn't hurt you at all!"

Betty exploded in an immediate flash of anger. "Hasn't hurt? How do you think I feel right now? Oh, you couldn't, you didn't, how could you?!" The angry tears streamed down her face as she ran into the bedroom, slamming the door behind her, and Bob heard the bolt slam shut. This was the first time he had ever been shut out of their bedroom.

After the explosion, they were quite distant for several days. The distance made Betty feel uncomfortable and she apologized for her stereotyped, tantrum-like behavior, and asked for lots of understanding. "You can't just throw off a lifetime of brainwashing in a few hours," she pleaded. Bob, for his part, was quite patient and accepting. He was so sure he had been right. "Betty is intelligent and inner-directed," he thought, "she'll agree."

The reader may be thinking that this is a peculiar outcome to a situation where, in our culture, the unfaithful spouse is the culprit who is supposed to feel guilty and beg forgiveness. It is important to recognize, however, that Bob and Betty represent an increasing number of people who also feel (1) a rational commitment to freedom, independence, and personal growth and (2) a keen desire for more honesty and gut-level sharing of their relationships with others. Betty's initial response to Bob's confession was the culturally-programmed stereotype of anger and indignation, in terms of transactional analysis, her Parent messages.

Ironically enough, Betty had not yet told Bob about Cal, who was out of town campaigning. "Anyway," she said to herself, "he's probably got a girl in every precinct. I'm really not expecting him to get back in touch."

But having faced the fact that she could let herself feel sexually turned on by other men and that she and her marriage could survive these feelings, Betty became more warm and radiant and very quickly attracted the interest of several men and two outright propositions. She turned each of them down for practical reasons. One was from a member of their social circle and a close friend of Bob. She thought that would make things just too complicated. The second was from a man with a shaky marriage, and Betty didn't want to become his excuse for divorce.

Nothing had happened, yet already openness about intimacy outside the marriage was working! Betty could call home now and say she'd be late, that she had met someone interesting and they were going to have coffee before she came home. Bob had another affair quite soon and admitted being involved, but denied sex. He still couldn't be completely open.

It was rough for months. There is no such thing as instant total openness. Within a year, each was telling the other about previous sexual experiences, ones that were over. They were not yet able to discuss what either did last night or this noon. In fact, they agreed to be discreet about current outside relationships if they felt they might be a threat. Bob told about a one-night stand in New York right after he came home because it was no threat. And they were on their way to freedom.

Six years later their life had shown how well openness about outside sex can work for some couples.

"I don't call what we do cheating or infidelity," says Betty. "I don't feel like I'm being unfaithful. Definitely not. In the first place, I'm being faithful to me and to what Bob and I agreed is best for us. In the second place, I'm being faithful to Bob, literally, because I do what I need to do to stay lively and sexy. And he needs me that way!"

"I'd rather have 80 percent of Betty the way she is now than 100 percent of the way she was before, good as that was," Bob says. "And about being faithful, sooner or later Betty will know about everything I've been up to. We're basically honest with each other."

"Besides, I really am a sentimentalist," concluded Betty. "I'd hate to look forward to growing old without Bob. There really is something to spending your whole life with a man, being able to look at the old snapshots together, having the grandchildren come visit, the whole old-fashioned bit! I look forward to sharing all the memories. And open marriage is great, because I won't have a lot of secrets I can't share with him. I won't be sitting across from Bob in my rocking chair thinking, 'If it hadn't been for you, you son of a bitch, I could have had a lot of fun—but now it's too late.' There must be quite a few old folks who look at each other that way. And I think it's sad. And unnecessary. I'd hate to grow old and still be having daydreams about this groovy guy I met once at a political rally, and how I should have said yes instead of no. My one big chance at a fling! And I blew it for Bob. The funny thing is that particular offer never worked out anyhow."

"That particular offer," Bob chuckles. "And speaking of offers, all this talk about sex is really getting me turned on. Isn't it about time for us to go home?"

These two are unusual, perhaps. But it is worth noting that their openness made all of the above conversation possible.

Bob and Betty's dog-eared copy of *Open Marriage* lies on the bedside table. By now, their eighteen-year-old daughter has managed to read it too. She likes the open marriage concept, including open companionship with friends of the opposite sex outside the marriage, but not including outside sex. Lisa points out that, with regard to outside sex, the O'Neills explicitly state that "such relationships are not necessarily an integral part of open marriage."

"I think the honesty bit is a groove," she says. "But I couldn't dig it if my man was making out with other chicks. So, like, he'd better come on straight with me but, you know, not about making it with other people. And if two people really groove on each other and really come on straight, they ought to be able to fly, man, without all that outside stuff. I mean, like, how much sex do you need, anyway?"

Betty and Bob listen carefully to their daughter. She reminds them of themselves twenty years ago. The syntax may have changed—but the idealism is much the same. They respect her attitudes, and they play it cool with her, keeping all the external images quite proper. For Lisa, her parents are an example of how great an open marriage can be without extramarital sex. Granted, her parents would be even more ideal if they could split the straight scene and get into organic farming or some other with-it endeavor! She has seen the lives of some of her friends tangled and upset by the divorces of their parents, and believes that adultery causes much of this pain.

Not that Lisa isn't cool about sex in the fashion of her generation. She definitely plans to get on the pill before going off to college in the fall, and has selected a campus with coeducational dorms. She feels she will want to have a number of close relationships—including sex—with different men before settling down. "Even then," she says, "I'd sure want to share a pad for a year or two before making any final decisions. And besides, why get married anyway? Like, if you really love each other and really dig each other, I mean, you wouldn't need any kind of formal ceremony to make you stay together, because you'd just want to!"

Lisa feels that her sexual striving is natural and good. She hopes, someday, to experience natural childbirth. She has no hang-ups about nudity and has posed for the life drawing class at school. She considers anything you dig to be a legitimate form of sexual expression, and marched with her lesbian friend in the Gay Pride Parade. Lisa also believes that an interracial marriage "would be okay, if you really loved each other a lot."

But while it is true that Lisa's sexual ideals differ somewhat from those of previous generations, she ultimately has as her ideal, and is looking for, a perfect, sexual pair-bond. If she sleeps around in the process of seeking such perfection, it's part of the search. At the same time, Lisa would like an open marriage, assuming, as she does, that a man committed to and in love with her simply would not need any outside sexual activities.

Many members of Lisa's age group move out into life with such passion and idealism about human relationships that it still seems possible to find the right person and, together, form an ideal couple who are totally sexually adequate for each other. This is obviously not true of all teen-agers and young adults. It's the just right solution—like winning without breaking any rules or asking any special favors.

Because Betty and Bob respect their daughter and her ideals, they have decided—up until now—not to tell her how they do in fact live. She is aware that they have an open marriage as described by the O'Neills but not that this openness includes, for them, extramarital sex. In their decision not to tell her, they have recognized that honesty has limits. They once considered the idea of an open family, but decided that in this one area at least (their outside sex), even a guarded honesty would be too threatening to the children. In fact, Lisa explicitly said, "If you guys ever did anything like that, please don't tell me about it."

Several more years elapse. Lisa is blissfully happy living with a man, and Bob and Betty's other children are in college.

But Bob recently suffered a slight stroke and has become much less active. He has gained weight, believes the slackness on the right side of his face makes him unattractive, and worries about his health.

Betty has remained trim, attractive, and vivacious. She receives many offers for dinner and weekend trips. Although she is now fifty-four years old, her vitality and love of living continue to attract men. She exudes enthusiasm, sensuality, and fun. She would still like to be involved in a totally open marriage, and misses sharing her exciting adventures with Bob. But since his stroke, it is all too obvious that he no longer delights in listening to them.

After this change in their life, Betty thought seriously about three options. First, she could leave Bob and seek a completely open relationship with someone else. Or she could give up dating and do only such things as she feels free to tell Bob. Or, finally, she could be as open as possible but remain sensitive to his needs, which is the true meaning of the O'Neills' concept of open marriage.

Betty decided on the third option. She realized that Bob needed her now more than ever. She wanted to be cheerful and caring around him. And she did not want to upset him with news he didn't want to hear. But at the same time, she recognized her extramarital adventures as a major source of strength and good feelings about herself that, in turn, enabled her to give Bob what he needed.

She knew she could no longer be fully open with Bob; openness about outside sex is an ideal which is no longer suitable for them. And not only that, already she had kept to herself how exhausted it made her to care for him around the clock the week after his stroke. And because he became so easily upset then, she censored some bad news letters from Lisa, which she was able to do because he liked to have them read aloud to him.

But Betty will be as honest as possible. This means she will continuously sound Bob out, gently pushing to learn just how much he can accept without being wounded. One night, when it was obvious she'd been out having a good time, he was eager to hear the details and seemed to enjoy them vicariously. But this interest in her outside life was but a flicker, and a few days later he said, "I'm really not interested. Just bring me some more tea and turn the radio up."

Now, he knows that she continues to go out, which they had long ago agreed to. She might say she is going out to a party with some friends. Being as honest as possible, she supplies as many details as may be appropriate without causing clearly distressful reactions. While she may not say she is going out for a sex-filled evening with a lover, she may admit that she is going to have fun and be with men, not just her girl friends. What she is doing is what she and Bob have agreed is right for them. She isn't preaching sexual monogamy and sneaking out for orgies. And she always leaves a number where she may be reached, even if indirectly through discreet and cooperative friends.

Betty is determined to give Bob all she can. But she is also determined not to totally restrict herself to caring for Bob without the outside activities that restore her spirit. "If I did that," she told a friend, "I'd start going downhill myself—and then where would we be?"

As for Bob, he would not want to think of himself as depriving Betty of what he knows she needs very much. But now, his reactions have made it clear that he no longer wants to hear the details.

This is one of the many situations that arise in the course of marriage in which openness must be modified—where one partner may remain enthusiastic and capable of openness, but the other gradually becomes insecure, threatened, or simply uninterested. When that is the case and one is determined to bankrupt neither himself nor his marriage, complete honesty is a luxury which everyone cannot always afford.

chapter 6

case histories: ems as a positive experience

We will describe some men and women who are deeply in love with their spouses, some who have comfortable but unexciting marriages, and others who are married in name only. Almost all of them have one thing in common: they enjoy extramarital sex. But they are not swingers who attend group sex parties with their mates or trade spouses with mutual consent. Nor is their story like Peyton Place with the melodrama of broken homes and ugly scandal. Just the opposite, the neighbors (and most spouses) of the persons we interviewed for this book would be surprised by their closely-guarded true stories.

We believe that the story of extramarital sex as a positive experience needs to be told. In sharp contrast to the popular view that extramarital sex is always destructive, we have interviewed scores of individuals for whom such experiences have had a positive effect on their functioning as parents, wives, and husbands.

The myth that our society is virginal before marriage and monogamous afterwards was exploded over two decades ago by the famous Kinsey studies. Our experience further challenges the widely promoted view that the ideal marriage for everyone is sexual monogamy with complete honesty between partners.

Our research interest is in the *quality* rather than the statistical *frequency* of extramarital sexual experience. We would like to know how extramarital sex (EMS) has affected Irene and Stanley, not merely how many Irenes and Stanleys there are.

By giving you examples of how married people do in fact reach out to find sexual partners for fulfillment, you can easily substitute less controversial activities and understand the broad concept of what we mean by reaching out. The following case histories tell about people we interviewed between 1969 and 1971 who, despite the taboos of society, decided that the risk–benefit ratio involved in extramarital sex was worth a try. Our concept of marriage gives sanction to this way of reaching out, so long as the participants remain responsible and sensitive to the needs of others.

Is this a scientific study? No. It is not a statistical study. Rather, it is a study of possibilities. To answer the question, Can a violet bloom? it is not necessary to find a million violets blooming. It is necessary only to find one. A single instance is sufficient to document a possibility. The possibility under consideration here is that extramarital sex can be beneficial to human beings in many dimensions of their personal lives and relationships. In this sense, we have found many violets blooming. Therefore, we tire of hearing doctors, ministers, and even marriage counselors insisting that violets cannot bloom.

The ubiquity of extramarital sex (EMS) among those whom we interviewed showed that it can be a positive, growthful, healthy, and nondestructive part of the lives of socially responsible and conscientious people. We are all familiar with instances in which EMS is handled carelessly; the results are messy; there are jealousies, fights, and broken homes. We all know that EMS can express a personal and interpersonal disturbance. However, our study forces us to recognize that these widely publicized, unfavorable case histories are only part of the story. The other part of the story is that extramarital sex can be positive. It can be related to maturity, personal growth, better marriages, and joy. Without denying the negative side, we feel a need to present the positive side of the story.

When we began our informal survey, we knew that many responsible, happy people were sexually monogamous. We were also aware that many irresponsible, unhappy people had sexual relations only with their mates. We were surprised to discover that some marriages improved when one or both partners engaged in extramarital sex.

We knew that extramarital sex in our society had intrinsically many risks and dangers. We also knew that sexual monogamy had risks, including stagnation, boredom, and deadness toward outside interests. We learned that to take the risks of EMS could help to avoid some risks of sexual monogamy. Extramarital sex may benefit the marriage, sexually and otherwise.

We thought that EMS meant that either the marriage or the marriage partner was inadequate, hence the person turned elsewhere for love and excitement. But we discovered that EMS occurs whether the marriage is good or bad. Often it fulfills needs which could not be fulfilled by any single relationship, within marriage or otherwise, no matter how perfect.

We believed that a feeling of guilt usually goes with extramarital sex. But we discovered that most of the persons we interviewed felt little or no guilt. And yet they were fully capable of experiencing guilt, for example, about striking a child, acting out of racial prejudice, and so on. Several stated, however, that they would feel guilt if, as a result of their EMS, they neglected their families, became hostile to the sexual advances of their mates, or destroyed another's marriage. But they took unusual precautions to avoid these outcomes. In fact, most felt themselves to be on the same team with their EMS lovers, with a real sense of respect for their obligations and marriages.

It is our hope that the following case histories will help to bring about a more honest evaluation of extramarital sex. The case histories are of people whom we interviewed entirely outside our own social circles: people we met on airplanes, in other cities, at meetings of all sorts. Our method was simply to ask questions. The cases we report are all people of middle and upper middle incomes, people over thirty years old. All are affluent and mobile. All but one live in large cities, suburbs, or near college campuses. One is from a small town. We were both surprised and gratified at the similarities of our reportable cases with those we rejected for reasons of discretion. This also added credibility to the study. We have changed the details but retained the gist of each story. We have used pseudonyms throughout. We make no attempt to call the results of our interviews an in-depth psychological study. We simply describe a lifestyle, and draw some conclusions.

Occasional, Casual Affairs

We found the occasional, casual affair to be the most common form of extramarital sex among those whom we interviewed. Below we present two typical histories—one a high school teacher, the other a business executive—each of whom described his marriage as good.

Jack

A thirty-nine-year-old high school physics teacher married for seventeen years, Jack sees himself as overweight and not having a great deal of sex appeal. But he has a warm, pleasant face and his eyes sparkle as he talks about his several affairs.

"Usually it starts out as a casual sex experience with someone I like. But it soon develops into a friendship with sex just one part of the relationship. These affairs have helped me feel much more tender and affectionate at home. I do have a good feeling of stability with my wife and children, without the frustrations of sexual monogamy.

"Yes, I've experienced times when a woman became too emotionally dependent on me. Then, I've had to end the affair."

Of course, the woman suffered. So did Jack. But who is to say they would have suffered less without the affair?

Jack now feels that this kind of suffering can be avoided by having EMS only with women who have roots. They have a firm commitment to their marriage, or if single, are deeply involved in a career and not looking for a husband.

"It's like trees," Jack said. "If two trees are firmly rooted, their branches can be safely intermingled. That's what I would call a responsible affair. But if a deep-rooted tree has its branches intertwined with a sapling and a strong wind comes along, the sapling gets pulled up. I have deep roots at home. So I've learned to pick women with equally deep roots. That way, nobody gets toppled. In fact, it's very pleasant."

Jack has also enjoyed intimate affairs without genital sex. He does not believe in the double standard, and accepts that his wife has the same rights, should she choose to exercise them.

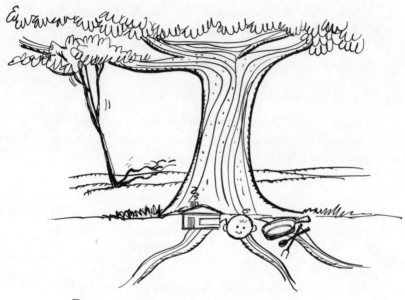

Don

After twenty-two years of marriage, Don describes his marriage as "absolutely great; a warm, close relationship with my wife and two children."

During the early years of his marriage, life was filled with gratifications at home, despite the presence of his chronically ill mother. At the same time, he felt pressured by the need to make it in the company.

But once he achieved business success and the children left home, he experienced a surplus of energy and warmth and simply not enough outlet for them. At the same time, he had more time and money. Typical of people in his wealthy suburb, sexual opportunity was everywhere, the risk minimal, the need for intimacy and variety growing, and so Don began having affairs.

There were a few awkward moments when his wife discovered he wasn't somewhere he said he'd be. But the years went on, and the marriage relationship continued to be great, according to Don.

Don said that he had never believed in the double standard, and very much wanted his wife to experience the joys of an affair. (Listening to him, you'd believe him too.)

When his mother's illness took a turn for the worse, so that she required round-the-clock care, the burden was crushing. "My wife needs a change," he told us. "I wish some handsome cat would just swoop her up and take her off for a passionate, romantic weekend. The nurse can take care of mother."

He honestly wants his wife to have an opportunity to get away and enjoy an interval of freedom from worry, and believes a romantic escape would probably be most effective. But there is no way that Don, being also involved with the burden, can provide this escape. He knows how much his affairs have helped him, and wishes she could enjoy the same benefits.

But his wife (a forty-five-year-old woman steeped in the habits and righteousness of sexual monogamy) probably could not handle a lover, even were he to appear. "It's too bad," the husband said. "I really wish she could. She needs something, and I can't think of anything else that could provide such real escape."

An affair need not be a threat to a secure marriage.

Controlled Response to Passionate Extramarital Love

We found examples of passionate extramarital love less frequently, but they definitely dispelled the myth that true love cannot be successfully handled as an extramarital affair. Here, each was a deep emotional involvement that did not destroy or demonstrably weaken anyone's marriage. We have included three case histories because of public resistance to accepting it as reality, not because we found it more usual than other types of affairs.

Delores and Lyle

For fourteen years, Delores enjoyed a secret, sizzling-hot affair with Lyle, a brilliant surgeon with an attractive wife, a good marriage, and two healthy children. Delores had married much too young, and speedily outgrew her accountant husband, whom she described as "cold and disagreeable most of the time."

Delores and Lyle never robbed their spouses of family-sharing time. Over and over again, they denied themselves the opportunity to picnic together on the beach, to go off together for a night or weekend. For fourteen years they have met almost exclusively for short periods in the afternoon, often using only their lunch hour.

Delores learned to make extra time in order to have time with Lyle without neglecting her family. For example, she organized her marketing so that she could be through an hour early, yet still get everything done. Then, instead of having coffee with a girl friend, she would meet Lyle.

Although we did not meet Delores's husband, we did get a glimpse of his waiting impatiently for her. He did indeed have an angry face, even though we finished the interview ahead of schedule. Delores kindly arranged for us to interview her lover. We found him very protective, and slightly hesitant to reveal his double life. He was most concerned about his status in the community, both social and professional. His reputation was impeccable and he was determined to keep it that way. Over and over again he said, "It is only because Delores asked me to . . . and I'd never refuse her anything." When asked about "anything," he quickly admitted, anything that would not jeopardize his career and his family. "It's just that I have so much faith in her, that she would never direct me to anything that would hurt me."

Lyle demonstrated no guilt whatsoever. He regarded himself as a good husband and father. He did not feel that his meetings with Delores had any adverse effects on either his family or his profession. Of course, it did take several hours a week during the day, but then he didn't play golf or ever indulge in long lunch hours. Between hospital rounds and starting his office hours was the usual time he met Delores. He maintained a special one-room apartment with a phone number known only to his secretary and answering service. "Delores adds great joy to my life," he said, "she really turns me on; seeing her adds so much enthusiasm to living. Of course it is frustrating, but I am very realistic. I will never leave my wife; I love her very much. Either I meet Delores discreetly and in a very limited manner, or I don't meet her at all." We suspect that his meetings are not all that secret to his close professional friends, but in fact do remain discreet since quiet knowledge is very different from gossip.

Who knows what Lyle's relationship with his wife would have been without this affair? We don't think it's possible to guess. Delores describes him as the kind of man who would have had another lover if not her, a man no one woman could satisfy. He wanted both the comfort of a wife and the excitement of an affair. With her, he had a cooperative, responsible, and discreet lover. With someone else, who knows?

As for Delores without this affair, she might have divorced and remarried. Again, it is impossible to predict.

Like other women we interviewed who are responsible and who enjoy EMS, Delores sacrificed other, common stereotype pastimes such as bridge to create time to be with Lyle.

We are convinced that Delores and Lyle were desperately in love, yet able to limit their relationship in order to function within the social structure.

It is possible to love more than one person at a time.

Anne and Michael

The idea of extramarital sex seemed absurd to Anne. Then, twelve years ago, when she was thirty-seven-years-old with only one of her three children still at home, Anne fell deeply in love with Michael.

As the months went by, Anne continued to resist sexual involvement with him. Meanwhile, he continued to offer gentle, open, and persistent invitations. Michael explained how to avoid pitfalls, and described all the positive joys. He was most understanding of her reluctance and never forcefully urged her to commit herself to a sexual relationship. To this day, Anne is not sure what straw broke the proverbial camel's back.

But after a year and a half, she began to meet him for sexual intimacy, and continued to do so two or three times a month for five years. Michael, we learned, had a better-than-average marriage and had been having outside sex for more than twenty years. He knew firsthand how his affairs added warmth and glow to his life. Anne was so impressed with his lifestyle. She loved him for being a considerate husband, for being so active in community work, and such a beautiful person all around. He was always punctual, very responsible; he just didn't fit into Anne's picture of a passionate lover. The first time Anne finally agreed to meet him in a hotel room, she had a marvelous experience. She admitted that that afternoon was the most exciting of her entire life. For the first time she resented his promptness as he jumped up at the designated hour to pick up his wife at work. She told us she was high for days. They continued to meet two or three times a month. Each meeting was ecstasy. And she considered the frustrations of limiting the ecstasy not too high a price. She often thought of her friends and neighbors—what would they think if they knew? Occasionally she wondered if any of them had secret moments of intimate joy.

The affair continued for about five years until Michael's business transferred him to another city. That was a real blow, she admitted. She confided in her best friend to have someone to share her loss. She then surprised herself by having a number of sexual encounters with persons she didn't know very well—she simply became available. "That lasted about two months," she said, "then I settled down." Now she has outside sex occasionally but has not had any experiences that could hold a candle to her super-sex with Michael. "It was a deep and passionate love," she said, "and it is hard to understand how one adapts. In some ways it seems like yesterday, in other ways like it was years and years ago. I wonder whom he is seeing now." She hears from him only occasionally when he is on a business trip. "But he never comes to Ann Arbor," she says, adding "maybe it's better this way. I can't imagine getting all fired up again for a single visit—oh, I'd do it; how I would love to see him—but the pain after would be rough." Anne is convinced he didn't love her all that much, but for her it was all-out being in love! "And still is?" we asked. She nodded.

History is filled with stories like this. Anne goes about her life with the joys and agonies of having experienced an intense love affair. When more time goes by, she will probably open up to more friends. She has no regrets whatsoever. Her life was greatly enriched. She accepts that there was suffering and frustration and now daydreaming. "But it was all worth it. I grew so much as a person. I feel much more mature and sophisticated. I understand the love stories so much better. My marriage is only mediocre. I might have gone through life without ever knowing what passionate love is all about. My major response is that I am grateful. Grateful it happened, and grateful that it didn't hurt anyone else. I never could have married him—that wasn't even a remote possibility. I feel I owe him a lot. Of course I would have loved to go off for a week, or even a weekend, or even one night. We never did spend the night together. But no one can take away what we did experience together."

Many feel that it is better to have loved and lost than never to have loved at all.

Fred and Ginger

Fred is a thirty-six-year-old auto repair shop manager. He has been married for ten years and loves his wife very much. For over a year, he felt turned on by Ginger—a strikingly beautiful and vivacious woman with a cold marriage. Finally, they arranged to meet alone.

Ginger is extremely passionate when they are together. But she continuously wrestles with the morality of her affair with Fred. She recognizes that it helps her feel alive and human and at the same time she is troubled by the contrast between her own experience and all the moral teachings she has heard. She repeatedly threatens to end the relationship, but as of our interview, it was still flourishing. Fred described it as a deeply emotional relationship that went way beyond sex.

Fred and Ginger meet in a motel with a common parking lot and a restaurant where Fred often goes. She parks her car at the shopping center several blocks away and Fred picks her up there. She has a bright red convertible and doesn't want it to be obvious near the motel. They worry occasionally about an accident and Ginger being caught in Fred's car the few blocks they drive together. "But," he said, "you can make up a crazy excuse once. After all, she works with me on a committee on Day Care Centers and I could make up a reason to see her, some mail to answer, problems with the phone company, and we decided to have lunch together. That would be it, though. We couldn't see each other again for many months. People don't swallow two goofy stories involving the same pair.

"We worry about this from time to time, but not so much as Ginger worries about herself. This affair is really tearing her apart. Sometimes I feel guilty. But then I ask myself—would she really be better off without me? I love her so damn much, of course, I'm not going to be overly rational. But she brightens up so much and she feels so great when we are together. She is unbelievably happy, then comes the time to go home. That's when she starts talking about religion—and how immoral we are. I've told her a dozen times, if she really believes that, we should face up to it and break up once and for all. I truly don't want to hurt her. But she is going to be hurt no matter what. I hate seeing her suffer. But she tells me how much these meetings mean to her; how dull the rest of her life is; how much she loves me. And well, I just don't know what to do. I feel great about everything except this damn religious guilt she has. I hear some people have affairs without this problem. I sure envy them. For my part it's beautiful. I feel high before, during, and after meeting with Ginger. I am getting used to her guilt feelings. I guess she is going to have them whether we continue or not."

Fred wouldn't identify Ginger or even ask if she would let us interview her. He became upset at the thought. "She'd die if she knew I was talking to you," he said, "she doesn't want anybody to know anything about us. She's scared to death. For me the affair is great and will fit just neatly into your histories of good sex outside marriage, but for Ginger it is a two-sided coin, with lots of turn-on and joy, but also lots of anguish. I just wish she could enjoy it with the freedom I do."

This torrid relationship between Fred and Ginger does indeed have its negative aspects, but the positive effect on Fred and his marriage came through so strongly that we decided to include it. Fred just beamed as he talked about how great he feels most of the time.

"My wife doesn't know why I'm feeling so good, but she likes me the way I am now, and my sex life at home is really better."

Extramarital sex may enhance the marital relationship.

Extramarital Sex and Ideal Marriage

In the above case histories, several EMS participants said "Yes, I love my husband or wife" and "We have a great marriage." In this section, however, we are describing persons whose marriages are even more ideal: passionate, exciting, and close. They speak of their marriages with such tenderness, warmth, and devotion that one quickly becomes aware that no one else could ever hold a candle to their spouse. Among these couples, we found sexual monogamy. And we also found extramarital sex.

We feel it only fair to present first two brief case histories which are exceptions in our presentation of EMS, for these individuals describe sexual monogamy as a truly positive and lasting experience. We simply wish to make it very clear that we do recognize this reality.

Bob and Gloria

Bob and Gloria have been married for sixteen years. Each acknowledges that he or she has felt temptations beyond marriage, but both partners were virgins before their marriage and neither wishes to risk any change in their unique relationship. They experience an exclusive, very private, very special bond. They feel exclusiveness adds a dimension to their relation which would be lost if either were to indulge in extramarital sex.

Seymour and Lois

Throughout their thirty-year marriage, both Seymour and Lois have enjoyed freedom in every area of life except extramarital sex. That is, they feel free to vacation separately, to enjoy different friends, and to pursue separate activities which interest them, but no sexual relationships outside of marriage. Each is pleased with this sacrifice made for the other and for their relationship. They now feel closer as two human beings than ever before. Each feels that their mutual sexual monogamy plays a significant part in this closeness, though it is by no means the dominant part.

Steven

Steven's marriage is right out of the storybooks. He describes it as ideal and loaded with enjoyment. During twenty-four years of marriage, he has almost never been bored with his wife. She is a typical home-loving soul. They live in a suburb of New York. He commutes into

Manhattan each day while she gardens, refinishes antiques, and prepares truly gourmet meals. Now in their late forties, they have sexual relations almost every night.

Steven's marriage is, in other words, just as ideal as Bob's or Seymour's. But that is only part of the story.

Steven has been an outstanding athlete since junior high school, not only on the court and field, but he's been a sexual athlete as well. He is not a Don Juan proceeding from one seduction to the next. He does not involve himself in one-night stands. And ever since his marriage, he has rarely had an affair with a single girl, and then only if she were firmly rooted in a career or other commitments. He is keenly aware of the danger of women-without-roots becoming too dependent on the affair. So virtually all of Steven's lovers have been married women who needed that special bit of extra attention, romance, or the mutual temporary ecstasy he could provide.

"I always explain how much I love my wife," he said. "It is important for me to make that clear. I become involved in affairs only as a supplement, an addition, not a substitute for any lack whatever at home. I simply have more need for intimacy and more sexual energy than my wife can possibly absorb."

To have denied himself the EMS and furthermore to have described his resultant frustration to his wife would have been honest, and also cruel. Had he even described the level of his sexual needs, his wife would have been miserable, for she prides herself on meeting his needs.

In meeting his own needs, Steven enjoys his dual role. He likes to enrich the lives of women who are, to some degree, unfulfilled at home, yet who are also strongly committed to their families. He feels that he has helped several women become more sexually responsive persons, and these women have told him that their sexual relationships with their husbands had improved remarkably because of this. "And they feel safe having an affair with me," Steven said. "They know I will never leave my wife for anyone else, and I will do nothing to disrupt their own marriage commitments."

Whenever he has sex with another woman in the afternoon, he always makes love to his wife that night, if she wishes to make love, making doubly sure he is not taking anything away from her.

His wife is equally open in her intellectual attitude toward sex, we learned when we interviewed her, but emotionally she is very possessive. "She would be deeply hurt if she knew about me," he said. "She couldn't imagine my sharing the kind of sexual closeness we have with someone else."

We asked him what he would do if he had a job where he had to punch a clock. "I don't know," he said. "I guess I'd just have to find another job." As it is, he is out of the office frequently on business, when he does not have to account for his whereabouts.

Because Steven lives near a large metropolitan city, he meets most of his lovers in large commercial downtown hotels. These hotels are hosts to business meetings of all kinds, and to be seen in the lobby or on the elevator is not in the least incriminating. He goes to the room first and then, at an appointed time, his lover calls from the lobby and the door is unlocked by the time she arrives. This minimizes standing in the halls, knocking on doors, or causing attention. On two occasions, he had prolonged affairs with women who had apartments that were available. But over the years, his choice for lovemaking was usually commercial hotels. In case there are readers who might think it unusual to book a room just for an afternoon, let us assure you it is not. Many salesmen book rooms for daytime use to display their wares and discuss important business transactions in private. Others book rooms for the same reasons as Steven.

When we talked separately with Steven's wife, she seemed very proud of her husband. She said she is "sexually satisfied and then some" and feels her marriage is tops. And we would agree with her. They both speak in glowing terms of each other, and they seem to be two of the luckiest people in the world.

Consideration for the feelings of others may require withholding the truth.

Frequent, Casual Extramarital Sex

In this section, we will be describing married persons who are firmly committed to their marriages as a first priority but also have had in the neighborhood of one hundred or more sex partners. Some experienced the majority of their casual sexual encounters before marriage. Others only developed the emotional freedom for casual sex after marriage. And of course, still others enjoyed casual sex before marriage and continue to enjoy it. Only the name has changed.

Because a person has many different sexual partners, the behavior is stereotyped as irresponsible, but we feel a need to stress that all of these persons were conscientious and socially responsible. These unique individuals appear simply to have the apparent freedom to participate in sex whenever and wherever a reasonably safe, attractive opportunity is presented, as long as it does not conflict with family, work, or other obligations. Their questions about potential sexual encounters seem to be: Is it feasible? Will it be enjoyable? Is it reasonably safe, so that my marriage will not be threatened?

By the time a person has accumulated this amount of sexual experience, the varieties of possible after-effects are well-known. Few men, but more women, admitted to having made some wrong decisions, but both were quick to add that there are no areas of life in which one can expect always to make the right decisions!

With rare exceptions, in those cases where the spouse knew of the EMS, spousal attitudes ranged from support to reluctant tolerance. In one instance, where the husband did not know of the EMS, his general strong hostility toward adultery implied that it might be utterly devastating if he found out the extent of his wife's sexual encounters. The critical attitude was attributed to his upbringing, reinforced by the mass media, sex educators, and textbooks that present frequent casual sex as the behavior of the irresponsible, the inconsiderate, the compulsive, or the neurotic.

None of the people interviewed expressed guilt about their outside sex per se. If given a chance to live life over, none would choose a sexually monogamous life.

Since our cases are select and limited, we eagerly await a more thorough study of frequent, casual sex. It appears to be relatively easy to find serious responsible persons who care about their families and are constructive members of society and who also participate in frequent, casual sexual affairs.

Corinne

Corinne is an extremely independent woman, yet very domestic and proud of her home and family. She has been married for seventeen years and has three children.

Her husband is dedicated not only to his work but to a number of causes, such as racial equality, guaranteed annual income, and free legal aid for the poor. Despite his admirable dedication and humane qualities, he simply could not be described as a warm and fun-loving person. In many ways, the marriage is cold. Sex occurs rather routinely. Corinne enjoys the love-making and rarely turns him down, even though their love-making falls far short of the ecstasy and abandon she is capable of.

Although Corinne often goes out on dates, she is very conscientious about arriving home at the anticipated hour, dinner is always ready on time, and so on. She told us how well her children do both socially and in their school work and, more importantly, that her children appear to be very happy. Although society would condemn Corinne as unfit to be a mother, this woman appears to be the model of vital and responsible motherhood.

Despite the relative coldness of their sexual relationship, Corinne respects her husband profoundly, is deeply committed to the marriage, and needs the stability he provides.

When asked how she so successfully was able to break away from tradition, Corinne admitted that her father was very radical in his ideas and believed in total equality for women, took life quite seriously, as does her husband, and worked hard to live up to his ideals. She also mentioned that her best friend, an unmarried woman who is a swinger, had introduced her to many other swingers. This friend has occasionally made her apartment available to Corinne for EMS. In addition, Corinne is a gifted amateur photographer and attends meetings and shows, when family obligations permit, and these times also provide an opportunity for discreet, casual sexual relationships.

She has had two serious love affairs, and both men eventually became her good friends, good friends of each other, and also good friends of her swinging girl friend. All four individuals are dedicated to two principles which we will summarize as (1) love without possession or exclusion and (2) love and let go. These are remarkable attitudes in a society which subscribes to exclusiveness and possession in its official attitude toward love and sexual behavior, beginning with going steady as early as the pre-teens and continuing into marriage.

Corinne simply washes away truly all notions about the evils of frequent and casual sex. Although her lifestyle indicates quite a different behavior, her attitude is one of a happy hooker. She doesn't believe there is anything good about sexual abstention. "And the reasons for abstention are so obviously arbitrary and irrational," she insists. "I'd love to debate the issue of sexual freedom; it would be so easy to win. Hell, I've had plenty of sex without intimacy and plenty of intimacy without sex. Feeling close and exchanging warm vibes, just feeling for the moment very close, very much on the same wave length with another person is real intimacy. People who are afraid to enjoy extramarital sex may remain intimate for years, but that creates lots of emotional strain on their families as well as on themselves. Are they pure because they don't have casual sex? Is their suffering good and their sacrifice noble? Who knows? Maybe one tumble with a lover might have ended the whole thing. You see, actually once you are sexually aroused, it can sometimes be very impersonal," Corinne recalled.

"In group sex, lots of times, you just close your eyes and are not even sure just exactly who is turning your body on. But it still feels good. And I apply the same value system to sex as to everything else. If it feels good and doesn't hurt anyone, it's great. There is nothing wrong with sex parties. Only those who want to enjoy them go. No one is persuaded to attend, no one asks whether or not others approve. So why put sex down just because it's not your cup of tea?" she asks.

"When I stand aside and watch a group tenderly enjoying sex in a hotel room and then think about the rowdy drinking with nudges, pinches, giggles going on in the bar downstairs, I wish I had movies with a double screen so middle-class America could see both at the same time—that which they label the evil of evils and that which they promote as a red-blooded way to relax and have a good time," she emphasized.

We could go on and on about Corinne. As for the time factor, the amount of time required for this activity, she answered, "We didn't spend any more time in the bedroom than they did in the bar!"

Margaret

Margaret is admirable in many ways, but she represents an exception to our cases where casual sex coexists with familial responsibility. Professionally, she is competent and earns a good salary. But apparently she is either not willing, or able, to respond to the needs of her three children. In conversation and probably in bed, she radiates a vital warmth. But she told us how poorly she communicates with her children. Divorced for over four years, she fails to come home at the expected hour, neglects to plan for their meals, and leaves the children alone without supervision. Margaret is quite openly defiant about the prevailing sexual mores and makes no attempt to hide her sexual activities.

Margaret, as a buyer for a large department store, needs to make many out of town trips. She makes no bones about sleeping around and talks of her boyfriends quite openly. In addition to the encounters she has in hotels, Margaret also invites men to spend the night at her apartment. She says that the children are so used to it that it doesn't bother them at all. What they do need, she admits, is a more motherly mother. Margaret has had only one serious affair since her divorce. Most of the men she meets she doesn't think are good prospects for marriage, so she simply has many temporary intimacies as a way to enjoy sex and feel a certain intimacy even if it's not with the same person very often.

Who is to say that she would be a more responsible parent without frequent, casual sex? Margaret is included in this series of responsible persons who enjoy casual extramarital sex because she is responsible professionally. To meet her, one would not imagine of her an uncaring and irresponsible mother. Perhaps she is one of the victims of a society that pressures women into becoming mothers. Perhaps without this American bias toward motherhood, Margaret would never have become a parent in the first place.

Clearly one can enjoy casual sex and demonstrate responsibility in some areas of life and not in others.

Stanley

A forty-eight-year-old traveling salesman, Stanley fits the sexual stereotype of his occupation. Stanley estimated that he has had over 200 sexual partners in his travels, all brief and casual. He insists he's had no really serious affairs.

Stanley lives in a small town and always returns with eager anticipation for the warmth and coziness of his home and family. He loves his wife, considers that he has a good marriage, and truly enjoys his infrequent relations with his growing children.

Stanley's lifestyle is an exception to the large city or university community. Since he lives in a small town, his extramarital sexual encounters are totally isolated from his home life. So is he much of the time. He lives in two worlds that are geographically apart as well as psychologically removed. Whenever Stanley goes away, he cruises around for pick-ups. He doesn't like to have to pay for sex. In fact, he has used a prostitute only once. He feels that there are enough women around who enjoy sex just for the fun of it. To date, Stanley has had no trouble finding women. Perhaps he will as he grows older. Maybe not. But Stanley takes his sex as he finds it, in a matter of fact way.

Frequent, casual sex may have little or no effect on the marriage.

Deborah

Deborah had an extremely active sex life as a teen-ager, with scores of sexual experiences, probably well over a hundred different partners.

Now, after twenty-three years of marriage, Deborah describes life with her husband as better than ever. When asked about extramarital sex, she said she feels no great need, although she would not turn down something very special. And she adds, "But it would have to be a damn good offer!"

Meanwhile, she is highly successful in her career as a newspaper columnist. She and her husband have a hyperactive social and cultural life: opera, ballet, art show openings, and theater.

Deborah and several other women whom we interviewed suffer no apparent repercussions from their teen-age antics.

Guilt and suffering are not the inevitable consequences of frequent casual sex in the young female.

Extramarital Sex as Forbidden Fruit

The next two cases involve persons who feel they have been deprived of warmth, love, and sexual response because of the prohibitions implied in traditional American sexual mores.

Lester

Lester, a sixty-eight-year-old man who has been married forty years, feels gypped. His only reward for a lifetime of sexual monogamy is incredible frustration, a keen sense of having missed warm, loving memories, and an abundance of a "What a fool I was" type of despair. He feels that he was led to believe all sorts of lies. But now, he thinks, it's too late to do anything about it.

When Lester remembers moments when he could have entered into meaningful love affairs but refused on the grounds of morality, he feels deep sadness and regret, even guilt, for having held back from life.

He and his wife have had no sexual experiences since he retired early over ten years ago, because of illness. The illness did not affect his ability to have sexual intercourse. It simply created a convenient time to end what had become dull anyway. We found him typical of many men and women in his age group.

Doing without extramarital sex does not guarantee future rewards.

Irene

Irene is keenly aware that she has lived for years in a home without love. But their friends view this woman and her husband as a good example of successful marriage. The two enjoy the same music, the same friends, and fishing. They plan a very special trip for each summer, plus small adventures in the spring and fall. Despite all this, Irene is emotionally miserable. Her husband has sexual intercourse with her often, but in a very routine manner, leaving her without satisfaction most of the time. Aside from the sex act (which is the proper term in this case), there is no cuddling or spontaneous touching between them other than, of course, perfunctory kisses when he leaves for work.

During her thirty years of marriage, Irene has broken out of the strict monogamy pattern twice, each time with such overwhelming guilt that she broke off the affair. One of these was brief but radiantly intense: "It made me so happy, I was afraid someone would ask what had happened to me."

Meanwhile, her investment in her marriage is so tremendous she feels caught. "I need love," she said, "but I can't live the lie of an affair."

Psychotherapy did not result in the husband's becoming more warm and understanding, nor were her own inhibitions against EMS loosened. The therapist's value judgment that "EMS can only be destructive and you should work harder on your marriage" was accepted by Irene because "Dr. Smith is an authority," even though her own experience contradicted his view.

The need for EMS may demonstrate a lack of warmth and understanding by the spouse. If a cold partner cannot change and one is not willing to divorce and EMS is desired but denied, is virtue its own reward? Irene says her virtue is not rewarding.

Some persons are blocked from achieving personal growth and emotional reward by strictures which they have internalized without a critical examination.

Extramarital Sex with the Spouse's Support

These are couples who support, not just tolerate, each other's EMS, but with different degrees of communication about specific activities.

Charles and Sylvia

"It hasn't always been this way," said Charles, "but after eleven years of sexual monogamy, our marriage was on the rocks and something had to give."

Married for seventeen years with four children, Charles and Sylvia openly discuss their extramarital sex, group sex, and homosexual experiences. Each has enjoyed sexual relations with many partners over the past six years, with the spouse expressing his or her knowledge and encouragement of the relations. Charles has had group sex, including experiences with homosexuals, but he has no hesitancy or shame in discussing these adventures with his wife. They feel that their marriage is secure and unthreatened by this behavior. They both have responsible jobs and are highly respected in their community.

"The first time Sylvie broke out of her cage into an affair, and then told me about it, I was so angry I smashed almost every dish in the house!" Charles remembered.

"Oh my God! What a night!" Sylvia agreed.

"But," Charles continued, "It turned out to be the beginning of a real relationship. I was suddenly face-to-face with my own possessiveness and fear of life. I had my foot on Sylvie's back. On my own back too, afraid to be honest about my own curiosity and desires. Well, we worked through these problems with a counselor for a couple of years."

"It isn't our new sex life that really has made the difference," Sylvia concluded. "It's that we've learned to let each other be, not to cling, and at the same time to relate honestly to each other. If this leads to extramarital sex and talking about it with each other, well, that's part of being human. Having experienced it both ways, I wouldn't want it otherwise."

Some couples openly accept extramarital sex.

Joe and Emily

Married for almost fifty years, Joe and Emily have, for the last twenty-five years, included another woman as part of their family. In addition to this special person, they have other special ones who share concerns and intimacies with them, sometimes with and sometimes without sex. The members of this larger family consult each other before making important decisions. They have changed jobs and relocated in order to live in the same city with other members of their family. The extended family have assisted one another in the rearing of their children. This is really not a group marriage, and has not been without its problems over the years. But among the participants, there is a deep understanding and loyalty, and a sharing of love and intimacy. Looking back over a half-century together, this couple remains deeply in love, and both feel self-respect for having lived according to their convictions.

An extended family can be formed by couples and individuals who care deeply about each other. This can include sexual closeness, contribute to the fulfillment of the family members, and extend loyalty, responsibility, and caring beyond conventional limits.

Glenn and Marcia

For Glenn and Marcia, knowledge of who the EMS partner is, is barely tolerable, but not an enthusiastic reporting of details. Married eight years, each agrees that affairs do happen and also agrees (at Marcia's insistence) to spare each other the specifics of who, where, what, and how good.

It didn't always work out according to this mutual agreement. Marcia's first affair was very destructive. She wasn't at home when the children returned from school, meals were poorly prepared, and she became hostile to her husband's sexual advances.

The couple has since relocated in another city, and Marcia has entered into a new affair which she is handling discreetly and responsibly. Glenn learned of it only after a year, and is not disturbed by it. He too has had several affairs during the eight years.

Glenn and Marcia agree that her first affair was destructive not because of her so-called infidelity but because of her obvious lack of concern at home and gossip in the community. They have lived and learned and now seem able to handle EMS in a context of family responsibility and mutual respect.

Many times, it is not the extramarital sex per se, but how it is handled, that is important.

Homosexual Extramarital Sex

Several persons were interviewed who are committed to their mates and families, and who have experienced varying amounts of homosexual EMS.

Ted

Ted is a forty-three-year-old man with a comfortable but unexciting marriage, a good sexual relationship with his wife, and an arrangement by which he has one night a week out, which he spends invariably with homosexual friends. He is grateful that he has been able to assimilate bisexuality into his life without a complex system of excuses and absences.

Lynne

Lynne warmly told of her pleasure in stroking the female body which she finds very attractive. "But," she said, "I don't feel turned on when I see attractive girls in public."

She states that her lesbian lovemaking started out as a group sexual experience, entered into more or less out of curiosity. She has also had several heterosexual affairs. She doesn't have any idea if she'll ever have another homosexual experience. It really is not that important to her.

Homosexuality occurs both regularly and irregularly among responsible married persons.

Extramarital Sex as a Growth Experience

Some people strongly feel that their EMS has helped them grow as human beings. They have become more sensitive to human needs and more aware of human potential.

Alicia

A woman who had a cool, though not hostile marriage, Alicia consulted a lawyer twice before she finally carried through her intention to divorce her husband. During the period of indecision, she had an affair with a married man. As she said, "It was stars and fireworks and the whole bit." But unlike other persons whom we interviewed, she was unable to transfer any of its after-glow to her marital relationship. Her lover's marriage was also just fair, but he had no intention of divorce because of the children, social stability, and other reasons. The point here is that her affair helped Alicia to make her own decision regarding the divorce. She did not get the divorce in order to marry her lover, but the strength and self-affirmation of the affair gave her the ability to decide. "I have more confidence in myself now," she said.

Extramarital sex may encourage the development of self-confidence.

Will

Over the Christmas holidays, Will took the children on a vacation trip. At the resort, he met a middle-aged woman (like himself) without her husband, whose children were the same age as his own. He described her as "warm, open, very easy to talk to." They soon found out that they had many other interests in common. She had experienced affairs before, and was definitely the manipulator. It wasn't until the fifth day that he recognized she had been gently urging him into bed.

Will could hardly believe himself! Born and reared a strict Baptist, he was a virgin when he married. His wife had a chronic illness with acute exacerbations and he would go as long as five years with no sexual outlet. He never masturbated.

Understandably, Will was frightened that he couldn't perform. He hadn't held a women close to him, let alone sexually, for over four years. And never in his life anyone but his wife. But his new friend reassured him that closeness was a rewarding experience in itself, and that the act of intercourse was not essential to a good feeling of warmth and intimacy.

He told us that he had never met anyone like her—good with her children, so responsible at home, and on her job—yet capable of affairs! He never had dreamed that anyone nice could have affairs without the slightest guilt. He has discovered many new values as a result of this experience and has gained a good feeling about himself. The growth experience went far beyond sex. "I have gained a sense of power, of self-determination. I don't feel so victimized by my home situation and I don't resent my wife's illness nearly so much.

"I feel I can handle nonsexual relations better now," Will said. "And who knows" (with a shy smile) "maybe I'll have another sexual one some day?"

Extramarital sex may uncover hidden human potential.

Evaluation: How Can EMS Help?

We have limited this chapter to a discussion of the positive effects of extramarital sex only because the negative aspects heretofore have been so widely publicized, while the plus side has been virtually ignored.

Unless one is so prejudiced that he or she regards extramarital sex as totally immoral even when it contributes to human happiness for all concerned, or unless one regards monogamy as moral even when it contributes to misery, one would be hard put to find fault with most of the persons whose case histories we've presented.

How is it that extramarital sex can enhance some marriage relationships and not others? We would not pretend to know all the answers. Based on our interviews, these kinds of things seem to happen:

Some people are discreet and considerate of their marriage partners, and are careful to keep their affairs from impinging on their marriages.

Some affairs provide temporary respites from problems at home. They provide new perspectives so the problems can now be solved or else lived with.

Some affairs help people to expand their sexual and relational repertoires when the alternative would be to feel stifled by the marriage and resentful of the spouse.

Looked at in perspective, some affairs are acts of kindness toward partners who are seriously ill, preoccupied, or exhausted by chronic problems—for whom the "should" of sexual or emotional response would be just one more burden.

Some affairs fulfill the felt need for a variety of sexual partners. A clear example is the bisexual man or woman for whom no single relationship can fulfill both desires.

Many affairs fulfill the needs of both partners in the affair, so that neither is being exploited by the other. An example is the temporary arrangement of two people who are each separated from their spouses for too long. How long is too long depends on the people.

A few affairs are just madness in the sense praised by Zorba the Greek—madness that some people need and that is clearly an exception to their usual routine—the exception, as it were, that proves the rule.

We would emphasize that on the basis of our case histories, extramarital sex is far less likely to preserve or enhance marriage when the spouse knows about it. This point is also confirmed by Kinsey in *Sexual Behavior in the Human Female,* as quoted later in this book. Show and tell often turns out destructively. But when a marriage allows some privacy and freedom for each partner with no questions asked, affairs stand more chance of working and benefiting the marriage. The privacy and freedom may be circumstantial—like out of town business trips. Or it may be an agreed on part of marriage.

We found extramarital sex co-existing with both good and bad marriages. It may simply satisfy needs that could not be met by any one relationship, no matter how perfect. Hence there is no reason for anyone who discovers that his or her spouse has extramarital sex to conclude, on that basis alone, that "My spouse no longer loves me," or "I have failed as a marriage partner."

If we can accept these facts, we may be able to work toward reducing the harmful consequences of such assumptions as that the uninvolved ("innocent") spouse is *supposed* to feel angry and jealous, and the involved ("guilty") spouse is *supposed* to feel ashamed and humiliated; or that the best thing is for the "betrayed" spouse to become "very brave and understanding" and the "prodigal" spouse to humbly beg forgiveness and promise never to err again. The most prevalent misguided assumption is that the extramarital sex *per se* is a primary cause of marriage failure, or, for that matter, of marriage success.

Some recent changes in our society increase the incidence of affairs. We can now recognize that some of these changes also make it more possible for affairs to be beneficial rather than ultimately destructive. The changes include:

Effective contraception and legalized abortion. Of the two, contraception is clearly preferable. But to know that abortion is there as a "fail safe" clearly makes a psychological difference. Perhaps it also makes an ethical difference in deciding whether or not to have extramarital sex, if consequences are a consideration. There are times when recourse to abortion probably makes the difference between an affair becoming destructive to the marital relationship, or not.

There are precautions to reduce the risk of venereal disease, and even if you catch it, doctors can cure it.

A contemporary lifestyle that for many people includes frequent trips away from home and the anonymity of large cities. This maximizes the opportunity for sexual encounters and increases the chance that discretion will prove successful. It gives circumstantial privacy and freedom to each spouse—both the one who goes and the one who stays home. Increasingly, they both go—to different places.

Today's nuclear family of just one man, one woman, and usually some children, puts more strain on the family than ever. Who is there to entertain and chauffeur the children, help with the dishes, listen to one's complaints, rub one's back, unclog the drain, and then make love? Just one other adult. If that can make you important to each other, it can also make you tired. If it makes marriage more important, it also makes marriage more likely to fail, for who or what can fulfill all those expectations? Either we think of ourselves as superpeople, or modestly agree with the French proverb, "Marriage is a yoke that sometimes takes three to carry." The psychiatrist O. Spurgeon English adds, "And conceivably, even four."

Transience—each year one out of five Americans moves. On the one hand, this makes spouses portable roots for each other; but on the other hand it accustoms people to establishing and breaking off relationships. For an increasing number of people, affairs seem to help them cope with this transiency. An affair is a way to enjoy some intimacy when there is too little: she goes ahead to her new job in San Francisco, he stays in Boston with the house and children until the school term ends. Either or both may have an affair in the interim. An affair can also be a way to enjoy some intimacy when there is too much. Not that there is too much intimacy at home, though that too might be the case, but that there is too much going on at home in terms of financial worries, moving plans, selling the house, and reassuring the children to enjoy the intimacy that might be there. People tend to get snappy at moving time and, for some people, it is hard to enjoy sex in a context that is a constant reminder of problems. But at such times, the release of sex may be even more needed.

Finally, rising expectations. We expect everything to get better and better—not merely income, employment, housing, and cars, but also personal relationships and sex. After reading some articles published lately, one would believe that at the least marriage should combine the intensity of a T-group with the excitement of an X-rated movie. However, some people seem to understand the limits of one person and one relationship and, rather than condemning their marriages as failures when these expectations aren't met, they seek some of this closeness and excitement outside the marriage.

Given these features of today's world, we believe that the professional involved in marriage-counseling is wise to recognize that extramarital sex can be helpful both to the individual and to marital relationships, even as he or she recognizes that EMS can harm other individuals and relationships. EMS may be a warm, exciting event and not a symptom of moral decay or emotional disturbance. The experience of extramarital sex may at times signal a shy and hesitant but positive step toward discovery, trust, and the risks of growth and love. Like a fawn venturing into the meadow, the least scent of disapproval sends one scurrying. Rather than frighten people away from life, we would throw our weight on the side of realistic and supportive evaluation. What are the odds that this outside sex partner will be responsible and discreet? What might some of the joys and sorrows be? Thus, if EMS is entered into or continued with full knowledge of its risks, the affair stands the greatest chance of being growthful, responsible, an experience of joy and self-worth. We believe that many of the ideas we have advanced in this book—especially dating after marriage and Compartment Four—can tip the balance toward a more positive marriage or new life.

Are sexually monogamous people happier or unhappier than persons whose lives include outside sex? There is no evidence that sexually monogamous couples have more or less fun in bed, or have better or worse overall relationships than couples in which one or both spouses enjoy outside sex. We doubt that such correlations could be established by research. And even if they were, there would be many individual exceptions—a few of whom we have described for you with honesty and care.

In a society where all public values are stacked against it, a warm human event takes place and its meanings and results may be a pleasant surprise to those who had expected otherwise. In the last analysis, we live as individuals—not statistics—and as individuals we must decide what is dispiriting or energizing or meaningful for us as persons, within our own contexts of morality and responsibility.

We are grateful to those persons whom we interviewed. Their openness, and their courage or curiosity or need to venture beyond conventional limits, has contributed to the search for truth. We are also grateful to our colleagues Don C. Shaw and Jerry Lama for their numerous insights into the relevance of these case histories. Finally, we wish to express our thanks to the publishers of *Sexual Behavior* magazine for including an adaptation of Chapter Six in the February, 1972 issue. The reader might be especially interested in the responses by David R. Mace, Ph.D., Gordon Clanton, James A. Peterson, Ph.D., Silas L. Warner, M.D., and John F. Cuber, Ph.D., which were published together with the article.

CHAPTER 7

BETTER DEAD THAN CAUGHT IN BED

A number of persons have reported to us that their nonsexual outside activities are limited and inhibited by their fear of sex, and/or by their spouse's fears.

For example, a woman is afraid to let her husband go camping in the Arizona desert for fear that he might meet an attractive local girl out there, and we know where that would lead! A man is afraid to let his wife attend a party without him, for he thinks she might meet an attractive chap there and, after too many drinks, end up in the sack.

Another man's wife urges him to get out of the house and do his own thing, but that person is *himself* afraid that he may become sexually and/or emotionally involved. So he stays at home.

And so it goes. The fear of outside sex is much more paralyzing and pervasive than it might at first seem. It not only inhibits actual outside sexual activity, but also blocks a broad range of other fun times, simply because they might conceivably lead to sexual involvements!

For that reason, we feel that it is important to deal openly with sexual fears, even if only to indirectly increase our freedom to reach out and enjoy life in nonsexual ways. And since any activity, even camping in the desert, might conceivably be an entree to sex, it is helpful to ask forthrightly: "Supposing activity x did lead to outside sex, what would be so awful about that?" If we can admit that occasional, responsible outside sex is not likely to bring the sky tumbling down around us, this can open up a lot of doors—most of which, despite our fears (or hopes) will not lead inexorably to sexual involvements.

This crippling fear of extramarital sex (or love) is dealt with helpfully in two books which we recommend. One is Dr. Albert Ellis's recent *The Civilized Couple's Guide to Extramarital Adventure.* The second, Dr. Marshall Bryant Hodge's *Your Fear of Love,* approaches the subject from a somewhat different perspective. Neither of these authors suggests that anyone must or should have outside sex in order to be a happy person—but they do explore many of the fears and fallacious reasoning that prevent many people from making decisions for themselves and reaching out for life.

It is often the case that one's fear of extramarital sex (or love) first surfaces with the discovery that one's spouse has had an affair, is having one, or is about to, and one then feels that this is intolerable and catastrophic.

Inspired by Dr. Ellis's rational-emotive approach, we will deal first with some of the common catastrophic expectations about affairs as they relate to the *spouse* having extramarital relations. (The basic thought process—with the conclusion that outside sex is an inevitably catastrophic event—is much the same whether applied to *your* sexuality or your partner's.) Of course, there is an element of truth in these beliefs and expectations about extramarital sex. In fact, affairs often, but not always or inevitably, are associated with unpleasant or destructive side effects. Nevertheless, we think we can show why these fears and dire expectations are more often than not irrational and unfounded, and thus a most untrustworthy guide for evaluating the possible advantages and disadvantages of extramarital adventures.

The knowledge that one's mate has had an outside sexual relationship may indeed be a most unpleasant discovery. You may very well wish it weren't so. But from a rational point of view, it is not intolerable, or unbearable, or an absolute catastrophe. It need not make you terribly unhappy, unless you continue to propagandize yourself by thinking about all the awful, catastrophic things that supposedly result from extramarital sex. Typically, these are:

1. *Extramarital sex destroys marriage.* In fact, it does contribute to the break-up of many marriages. But sexual experience does not break up the marriage, the couple does, through the interpretation they make of the extramarital sex, as well as many other aspects of their life together. However, remember that, until recently, the considerable evidence that extramarital sex has actually helped many marriages has been suppressed. Whether it helps or hurts you, your spouse, or your marriage is up to you.

2. *My spouse's extramarital sex means that our marriage has failed.* It may in fact mean that you have had a bad marriage. But the existence of outside sex does not, by itself, prove that your marriage isn't working. It may mean no more than that your spouse is experiencing a growth time and that, given a chance, your marriage can also grow. And based on our own case studies, an unhappy or bad marriage is only occasionally the reason for an extramarital affair.

3. *My spouse's extramarital sex means that I'm a lousy lover.* The word "different" is probably more accurate than "lousy," since there is a great deal of anthropological and sociological evidence that a variety of partners is a sexual turn-on for most people.

4. *He or she has betrayed a trust and broken a promise.* The traditional words by which most of us were married contained the phrase, "forsaking all others, till death us do part." This is generally taken to mean (1) that sex will be limited to marriage and (2) that there will be no divorce. But unless these expectations were clearly spelled out in so many words, it is usually the case that you and your spouse just said the words because that's what most people say when they get married. That is not to imply that you didn't really mean them. However, when and if it comes to divorce with the possibility of remarriage, only the Roman Catholic Church forbids it. In

most other religions, divorce and remarriage are allowed. The marital *intention* is for a lifelong marriage, but circumstances often intervene, a fact which most religious bodies wisely recognize. Literal interpretations of ceremonial vows are not always human interpretations.

But assuming that the words do mean no sex outside of the marriage, here again, as in the case of divorce, many clergymen and others are taking a different view. For example, *Towards a Quaker View of Sex,* written by an official committee of the Society of Friends in England, 1963, states:

... The state of mind that ensures loyalty to the marriage partner may in fact shut other people out from the warmth and friendship they need. Morality may be achieved by "working to rule," but at the cost of depth and understanding; among the unmarried, chastity may be upheld at the cost of charity towards those in different circumstances.

Thus, the feeling of a literal betrayal based on the words of the traditional marriage vows may be what the Friends call "working to rule, but at the cost of depth and understanding. . . ."

Understanding and depth require, then, that you inquire into the meaning of outside sexuality in the life of your spouse. If, as a result of it, he or she has grown as a person and/or has become a more pleasant and worthwhile companion for you, then the literal act of extramarital sex may be just the opposite of betrayal in the true meaning. In that regard, we like the thought from the musical comedy, *Kiss Me Kate,* that one can be true to one's darling, in one's own fashion and way.

Other portions of the traditional marriage vows have gone by the boards, as well. For example, how many women today can say *and mean* "to obey"? In these days of women's liberation, very few would place a literal meaning on those words.

On the basis of our own case histories, we can conclude that very few people enter into outside sexual relationships in order to betray their spouses.

Therefore, it is irrational to go on indoctrinating yourself with the idea that extramarital sex is a betrayal. As the Quakers say, this is "working to rule, but at the cost of depth and understanding."

5.   *Things can never be the same between us again.* This feeling is, in part, based on the five items mentioned above—that since outside sex destroys marriage, that means our marriage is bad and I'm a lousy lover, and I have been betrayed, how could he or she do this to me? Of course, things can never be the same. Hopefully, things may be better! That is not a guarantee, but it is a possibility. We know of instances in which extramarital sex, when discovered by or reported to the spouse, has led to an opening up of communication—some of it painful, some of it beautiful—which helped to elevate the marriage relationship to a new and higher plane. Obviously, this doesn't always happen. But it can, if you and your spouse are open to the possibility, and refuse to be indoctrinated with the old standards, irrational thoughts about outside sex that have hopefully been put down in the preceding paragraphs. Often, having discovered that your spouse has been having an affair, and then looking at the marriage objectively, you will recognize that your marriage is already in fact better, and the improvements date close to the beginning of your spouse's affair or affairs. We are not saying that if your marriage has been improving, an affair must be the reason why. And we are definitely not urging anyone to describe their extramarital sexual exploits to a spouse on the outside chance of a positive breakthrough, for as Kinsey and his colleagues stated in 1953 in *Sexual Behavior in the Human Female:*

. . . there are cases of extramarital activity which do not seem to get into difficulties. There are strong-minded and determined individuals who can plan and control their extramarital relationships in such a way that they avoid possible ill consequences. In such a case, however, the strong-minded spouse has to keep his or her activity from becoming known to the other spouse, unless the other spouse is equally strong-minded and willing to accept the extramarital activity. Such persons do not constitute a majority in our present-

day social organization. . . . Extramarital relationships had least often caused difficulty when the other spouse had not known of them.

Finally, we do recognize that outside sex engaged in by irresponsible people often has unpleasant, and sometimes destructive results.
However, we suspect that a great deal of the destructiveness comes from
action based on the dire expectations we have been discussing—all of
which have some objective and rational components, and all of which
are usually irrational, nonhelpful attitudes. In that regard, we again
quote the Kinsey study with italics added for emphasis:

> In a culture which considers marital fidelity to be the symbol and
> proof of such other things as social conformance, law abidingness,
> and love, many of the females had found it difficult to engage in
> non-marital sexual activities without becoming involved in guilt
> reactions and *consequent* social difficulties. The females who had
> accepted their extramarital activity as *another form of pleasure to
> be shared* did not so often get into difficulties over their extramari-
> tal relationships. . . .
> Some of the extramarital relationships had been carried on for
> long periods of years without ill effects on the marital adjustments;
> but *when the other spouse discovered them,* difficulties and in
> some instances divorce proceedings had been immediately begun.
> In such instances, the extramarital coitus had not appeared to do
> as much damage as the knowledge that it had occurred. *The diffi-
> culties were obviously compounded by the attitudes of our culture
> toward such non-marital activity.*

Thus, it is precisely the irrational attitudes of our culture we use
as self-fulfilling prophecies that actually cause the dire expectations to
happen!

We also recognize that the chances of an affair being a positive
experience depend on its being an informed decision. A serious consideration in deciding whether or not to enter into an affair is the fact that
most affairs don't just fade away. When the relationship ends, there can
be trauma. And we're in favor of facing up to the fact that the vast
majority of affairs do come to an end. It is the case, without being sexist
but simply reporting facts, that more women than men experience deep

trauma at the end of affairs. The question then becomes: Is it worth it to establish ties, even though that will mean tears and anguish when we finally say goodbye? That is an individual decision.

We have reviewed five rather common dire expectations about extramarital sex from the point of view of the spouse who has discovered or has been told that his or her mate has been, or is, having an affair.

It is important to point out, however, that the person having the affair may very well be telling himself or herself the same things: "It will wreck my marriage, it must mean my marriage is bad and that my spouse is not a good lover, I am doing something terrible to my spouse, and I am a lousy, good-for-nothing for betraying a sacred trust. This must be so because that is what affairs indicate."

Who says so? Not these writers. Our many case histories indicate that these are not the quid pro quo implications of an affair, yours or anyone's. Therefore, reread the above five points and the arguments against them. Think of your own experiences and develop your own arguments against them.

This is especially important with regard to "it must mean my marriage is bad and that my spouse is not a good lover." The person who really believes that, either as a fact associated with affairs or as a rationalization to escape the bad rap implied by the other points, often will start "seeing" evidence that the marriage is, in fact, bad and the spouse is, in fact, poor at making love. Again, this may be largely a self-delusion. An outside affair often seems better when in fact it is just different. But suppose that the outside sex is in fact somewhat better. This is not very surprising, if you consider that you and your lover don't have to contend with mortgages, dirty dishes, and children. Many people who get divorces in order to marry their lovers don't stop to consider the very important differences between most marriages and most affairs. As for your being a dirty rat and a marriage wrecker, that doesn't depend on the affair as such but on how you handle it. If you are a responsible, nonexploitive person in most areas of life, you will probably be a responsible nonexploitive person in the context of an affair. It is highly probable that you can handle some passion without losing your head and messing things up.

Finally, we would say just about the same things to anyone contemplating outside sex. If you are a generally responsible, discreet person, your dire expectations, if you have them, will probably not come to pass. In addition, there is no certainty that those activities you fear will lead to sexual involvements will in fact do so—unless you decide, on the basis of further information, that that's what you want.

Like most everything else in life, the value of extramarital sex— whether for good or ill—depends almost entirely on how it is handled by the individuals involved. It is neither the enemy of all that is good and decent, nor is it good in and of itself. Outside sex can be a straight-forward affirmation between two people who like each other very much. Or, on the destructive side, it may be part of a game where the pay-off is to hurt third parties. It may be just fun for two people—nothing very deep and no hidden agendas. It may fulfill curiosity about what sex is like with different kinds of people. Or it may be a search for a new marriage partner. Outside sex may fill a void of loneliness and desire when one's spouse has been ill or gone for too long. Or it may be a simple sexual release after periods of enforced abstinence. And, at times, it may be a flight from real intimacy—diluting relationships so that none of them are too important. Or it may satisfy a need or desire for a kind of sexual activity one's spouse doesn't enjoy. At one time it may be one thing, at another time, something else for the same person. But one thing is clear: extramarital sex does not have to lead to catastrophic consequences. It can be an opportunity for just the opposite.

We evaluate sexual monogamy by the same standards. People who are sexually monogamous sometimes express fear about trying something or someone new. Or the reason might be loyalty—as one understands loyalty—to someone you love very much. Sexual monogamy can also be part of a blaming game: "I am sexually unhappy and it's all your fault!" If a person is free to seek different partners, and still remains sexually unhappy, it then becomes his or her personal hangup. Sexual monogamy also can be representative of a marriage relationship that is unusually fulfilling. On the other hand, flashing the wedding ring as a defense against extramarital relations may be withholding love from someone who needs it: "I can't, because I'm married." Sexual monogamy can be a satisfactory relationship for people with low or similar sex drives and tastes. Or it can be a strain for people with contrasting sexual drives and desires. Sexual monogamy, like extramarital sex, can be interpreted in more than one way.

Not only does extramarital sex have different meanings at different times for different people, but it is engaged in by persons whose marriages differ greatly. It is too easy to speak of extramarital relationships as though there were certain givens in every marriage—including such basics as appreciation for each other's needs and wants. For in many marriages, there is little such appreciation. (However, as we pointed out above, the existence of extramarital sex or desire for extramarital sex does not by itself indicate that anything is lacking in the marriage.) The hassles of making a living, managing a household, and raising children tend to interfere with intimacy and sensitivity. Another given that is assumed by many is that most couples enjoy a more or less satisfactory sexual relationship. But the reality is that many couples have miserable sex lives. (Again, outside sex does not necessarily imply that sex life is bad at home.) Other couples are making love joyfully almost every day after thirty-five years of marriage—and according to our case histories, some with outside sex and some without. Whatever the pattern is, the chances are that sex for many marriage partners happens either more or less frequently than they would choose. This is not to say that they must have extramarital sex to be reasonably happy people. But it might be an added dimension and increase life's joy. It would be exceedingly rare that two people over a period of ten or twenty years would continuously have the same appetite for coitus with each other. And it is our educated guess that millions are forced into a pattern of infrequency of or abstinence from coitus at times when sex is very important to them. This means years of frustration with solitary masturbation as the only regular sexual outlet, and for some, even this is excluded.

There are low-key, low-energy people who do not find life very exciting either inside or outside of marriage. There are high-key, high-energy people who find both marriage and outside activities exciting and rewarding. There are marriages where the partners have had their fill of sexual variety before marriage, and others where variety and curiosity are unfinished business for one or both partners. There are couples for whom role-playing is important: the wife does wifely things and the husband does husbandly things. For other couples, roles change. The basic role of breadwinner may be reversed. Also, there are structured marriages with musts like sex every Saturday night as well as those marriages where things are more spontaneous. There are marriages with children and marriages without them. There are marriages with serious financial problems, drinking problems, health problems, and those with no clearly discernible problems.

In addition to all these variables, there is another. The partners in many marriages tend to grow at different rates in different directions. Interests in various hobbies, persons, and pursuits may appear long after the marriage vows are sealed. And at the same time, some activities that once provided hours of common pleasure may now have lost their appeal to one or both partners.

Therefore, various strategies advanced in this book are designed to loosen the bonds and the "three-legged race" aspects of marriage. By allowing each partner a private compartment in which to do his or her own thing, we believe many marriages will become more viable. Within the limits of basic responsibility, Compartment Four allows for fulfillments and opportunities for personal growth that the marriage does not, or cannot, provide. In short, Compartment Four marriage does not ask the partners to grow dull to fit the marriage. Compartment Four marriage also puts sex into perspective: it may include outside sex—but it may also include outside chess or outside belly dancing, or a host of other outside activities that don't fit comfortably into the marriage or are unacceptable or annoying to the spouse, without ever including outside sex at all.

Independent decision-making is most feasible in the urban areas where three out of four of us now reside—in which most middle-class persons have a degree of mobility, affluence, and anonymity unheard of in rural towns and villages a century ago. The three "ps"—pill, penicillin, and pad (apartment) mitigate against the risks of pregnancy, disease, and discovery. Given these presentday realities, the fear that outside sex must be catastrophic and destructive is indeed an irrational one. But again, we want to point out that outside sex is not a *sine qua non* of liberated marriage, but simply one of many options for those who want it.

There are additonal features of modern society that help to explain why more and more people are engaging in outside sex. (Since the Kinsey studies were published, we have known that intimacy these days is not very exclusive and that a majority of Americans become involved sooner or later in one or more extramarital affairs.) One feature of our society in the last half of the twentieth century is that the extended family of the past has all but disappeared. Grandparents, aunts, bachelor uncles, and other assorted kin no longer share the home and responsibilities.

In addition, every year one out of five Americans moves. The executive mobility rate increased 500 percent between the end of the Korean war and 1969. Also, as of 1969, 73 percent of the Massachusetts Institute of Technology class of 1963 had already left its first employers. Popular quips are that "I.B.M. really means I've Been Moved" and "the definition of an optimist is the man who brings his lunch to work at Boeing." So we see the Ruths and Bobs of our age moving from house to house, suburb to suburb, shopping center to shopping center.

Dr. Warren G. Bennis has called this pattern "the temporary society," in an article of the same title that appeared in the *Journal of Creative Behavior,* Fall, 1969. Our society is one in which jobs, addresses, and human relationships are increasingly temporary. Dr. Bennis sees us as moving into and out of a series of temporary relationships— never quite in phase with one another—so that by the time one person is ready to say hello, the others are packing their bags. He suggests the the musical theme for our society is the Beatles' "I say hello, you say goodbye. . . I wonder why I say hello and you say goodbye."

Relationships in the neighborhood, at church, and at work are formed and broken off quickly. One feels an urgency to make friends quickly and relationships are often kept casual or superficial, perhaps so it won't hurt quite so much when it's time to say goodbye. Dating clubs, singles bars, and swinger's magazines facilitate instant introductions. However critical one might be of such contemporary institutions, they do seem to be a response to the mobility which repeatedly spirits away one's friends and associates. If you move slowly in finding new friends and intimates, you or they will already be moving away by the time you get close.

However, there is typically one ongoing relationship: marriage. Thus, as Bennis suggests, marriage becomes "portable roots." This tends to make marriage more important; hence we place more demands on it. Expecting more from marriage, we are more often disappointed. Spouses are expected to be lovers, best friends, and mutual therapists. The outcome is ironic: marriage "is increasingly likely to fall short of the demands placed upon it and be dissolved," Dr. Bennis said. The rising tide of divorce indicates that people are expecting more from marriage than it can deliver.

With the demise of the extended family, it is probable that marriage needs to be supplemented somehow if it is to survive at all as a viable form of human relationship. Communes seem to be an attempt to restore the extended family. Agricultural communes recreate a relatively nonmobile and traditional way of life. Group marriage is another option being explored. However, we do not foresee a time when these lifestyles will become dominant. Therefore, most of us will need to create other ways to find the intimacy that makes life worth living. Those of us who move often will need to learn to develop ties quickly, savor them deeply, and let go gracefully when the time comes to say goodbye.

And even if the family is to some extent portable roots, we have sincere doubts that so small a unit can fulfill the needs of its members for a variety of human relationships. Many who believe it can or should fulfill these needs often engage in outside sex as a search for a new partner who can do it all, that is, one who can meet the gigantic expectations of exclusive-possessive marriage. Of course, wrapped in the high expectations are already the seeds for the next divorce and the next. This pattern—serial monogamy—changes partners rather than expectations. We believe it would often be more rational and beneficial to change some of the expectations.

At this point, we offer the following analogy to the role of Compartment Four.

Each person might be said to live on a Home Planet. When you were a child, you probably shared your Home Planet with one or two parents plus siblings, if there were siblings. Other kin may have shared it.

At the age of five or six or so, an additional planet came into your life: the School Planet. At the age of twelve or sixteen or so, you also began spending time on a Work Planet. Each of these planets exerted more or less gravitational pull on you. And there were other planets, too.

Somewhere along the line, it is likely that you began visiting a Private Planet. You did not share what happened on your Private Planet with teachers or parents. The Private Planet may have been an abandoned barrel in the dump where you met your friends to look through girlie magazines, exchange jokes, play doctor, and so on. You may have enjoyed an unusually open and accepting family, so that a Private Planet was virtually unnecessary, or small and seldom visited. This can also happen in *some* unusual marriages. And at some point, if you are heterosexual, you began to share your Private Planet with those of the other sex. If you are gay, the Private Planet was perhaps even *more* private, due to cultural factors. Private, of course, means with respect to certain individuals.

Being a denizen of our culture, you were programmed to believe that sooner or later a romantic escapade on your Private Planet would lead to the establishment of a new Home Planet. And also according to our cultural expectations, at that point you would cease to have a Private Planet. To make a new Home Planet, one had to give up Private Planets, they said—and especially with regard to romance, intimacy and sex. Everything, now, would be shared with your Home Planet Partner (HP Partner, for short).

If you were a student, you could still visit a School Planet. But you would tell your HP Partner all about it if asked. And there would be Work Planets, and perhaps others. But there would be no secrets about them, either.

Some people even said that the more time you spend on your Home Planet, and the less time you spent on other planets, the better life on your Home Planet with your HP Partner would be. Life on your HP would be so wonderful that you would never want to leave it, ideally speaking, of course. And you believed them.

Let us suppose that after several years on your new Home Planet you felt a strong urge to make pottery. You knew that would give you so much pleasure! "Wet clay smells earthy, and feels so good in one's hands," you thought. But you explored hither and yon, and found no clay deposits at all on your HP. How disappointed you were—especially when you looked in the Law Book, just to be sure, and found: "If, having selected a new Home Planet and a Partner to share it, you find certain materials lacking, you must do without." A list of the "certain materials" followed and, alas, clay was on the list.

But still you dreamed of clay, and wondered if there was a nearby planet that had clay. Perhaps it wasn't so much that you needed pots, for your HP had metal to make containers. You just dreamed of the smell and texture of moist clay and the pleasure of molding it. And you felt angry that you had no clay, and angry about the Lawmakers' rules.

Meanwhile, children were born to you and your HP Partner. You and your partner cleared and planted, and added to your house. As your HP became more beautiful and wonderful, you realized that its gravitational field was increasing: each morning when you blasted off for the Work Planet, you were using more fuel than the day before! And each afternoon when you returned, you could switch off your rockets further out in space and depend on gravity.

Of course, despite your HP's increasing gravitational field, you still had plenty of rocket fuel to blast you on your way to work. This fuel was what they called "Liquified Sense of Responsibility," or LSR Fuel, for short. Most denizens of the culture were given a great deal of LSR Fuel when they were children. The rule was that "LSR Fuel may be used only to propel oneself to and from Home Planets, Work Planets, School Planets, and other Approved Planets."

Still, you dreamed of clay. One day at work, you made a new Friend. It could have been a he. For our story, let the friend be a she. And so your Friend confided that she loved to play with clay. In fact, there was lots of clay on her HP. But her HP Partner loathed clay. "It's so sloppy and messy," he always said. "You get it all over yourself and all over me. And I don't like the earthy smell."

"So you're unhappy?" you asked your Friend. "Oh, no!" your Friend said. "I know another planet with clay. It's nearby. You and I could go there after work and have fun!"

"But I'm afraid I'd have so much fun I wouldn't want to go home," you said. "And that might lead to you and I wanting to make the Clay Planet our Home Planet and live there together. Not only is it wrong, as the Lawmakers say, but I would miss my Home Planet. Even though it has no clay, it has wood and metal and my HP Partner, whom I love, and our beautiful children."

"Oh," said your Friend, "don't you have any LSR Fuel?"

"Of course," you said.

"Then use it, like I do!" she said. "Don't forget, I have a Home Planet too. Sometimes after work I go to the Clay Planet with friends. We play for awhile. Sometimes I even go by myself, but it's more fun together! You see, I have lots of Liquified Sense of Responsibility, and my HP has a big field of gravity after all these years and is very bright, so I never have any trouble getting home."

"You mean you trust your LSR Fuel that much?" you asked.

"Certainly," said the Friend. "The Lawmakers say you can't, but I tried it and, for me, it always works."

"But," you said, "I have heard of people who went off to play on other Planets and didn't go back to their HPs."

"That's true," said your Friend. "However, some Home Planets have almost no gravitational pull at all. Sometimes I think it's because they are new HPs without houses and loyalties and other ties. And of course, don't forget Anti-Gravity!"

"Anti-Gravity?"

"Certainly!" said your Friend. "You know, when HP Partners do certain things, it starts building up Anti-Gravity. For example, clay disgusts my HP Partner and he dislikes people who play with it. When he picked our Home Planet, I thought it was because he liked clay! I didn't ask—just assumed, you know. Well, it was just wishful thinking. Anyway, if I told my Partner I went to the Clay Planet with a friend, that would make him very angry. That would add Anti-Gravity to our HP. Or if I called him names, it would. Or if he struck me. And once your HP has too much Anti-Gravity, it takes almost more LSR Fuel than most people have to get back—even from their Work Planets! So, since

I like to be able to go to the Clay Planet with friends and still get home, I try to keep the Anti-Gravity low. Does your HP have much Anti-Gravity?"

"Almost none," you said. "Except, when I think about clay, sometimes I get very sad. Sometimes, I get angry at my Partner, even though it isn't anyone's fault."

"A pity," your Friend said gravely, "for that adds to the Anti-Gravity of your Home Planet."

You thought about that, and began to think that maybe she was right.

Every day thererafter, your Friend at work sent you little notes that said, "Let's play in the clay today." And whenever she passed you in the hall, she said, "This afternoon?"

And still, you didn't go. You were afraid that the Lawmakers were right—that something strange would happen, that your LSR Fuel wouldn't fire, or your Home Planet would suddenly lose its gravity, or some other natural law would be suspended.

But your Friend didn't give up. One day you came in, and right in the middle of your desk was big glob of moist, gooey red clay. The note said, "I know where there's more!"

Suddenly, wanting very much to go, you had a memory flash—of childhood afternoons on your Private Planet. "Why can't I have a Private Planet of Personal Pleasure now?" you asked yourself. "A Private Planet of Red Clay! It can be private from my HP Partner, so I won't say things that create Anti-Gravity on our Planet."

And, to make a long story short, so it was.

Note: It has been observed that marriage has three components: "me," "you," and "us." The Home Planet does not represent the marriage partner. Instead, it represents the "us" that exerts a gravitational pull on both partners, and shines its light into the sky to guide them home, regardless of how similar or dissimilar are their travels, what they do "out there," or with whom.

We hope that the little story about the planets is helpful in contrasting traditional with Compartment Four marriage. In Compartment Four marriage, each partner is entitled to a Private Planet for Personal Pleasure. It's just another way of saying Compartment Four.

There is an additional feature of our temporary society—the fact that marriage, although promoted as necessary, is no longer a procreational, sexual, economic, or social necessity for society. We maintain that this is the fact, regardless of remarks made by others that "the family is the foundation of society" and so on. Perhaps you will disagree. All right. But at least, consider the following brief items:

1. In an overpopulated world, procreation is only minimally necessary. If only 10 to 20 percent of the people in their reproductive years in the decades ahead reared children, that would be more than enough. Hence, marriage is not needed as a widespread arrangement for the production and rearing of offspring.
2. It need scarcely be mentioned that in today's world, marriage is not a sexual necessity, for sex of all kinds is rather easy to come by and with little risk of pregnancy or disease for responsible persons who take precautions.
3. Marriage is no longer an economic necessity. In the days before sophisticated technology and industrialization, 90 percent of the people were farmers and their families were working units. But today, it is the individual, not the family, who is hired by the large corporations and institutions for which most of us work. Many women, however, find marriage a great economic advantage. Children rarely see their parents at work. Except in the sense that many employers are still prejudiced in their hiring practices, preferring married to single people, marriage has little economic importance other than as a consuming unit.
4. At a time when sexually active unmarried persons are becoming accepted by society, marriage is no longer really a social necessity. It is probable that most people these days can have more sex, more friends, more freedom, and, for women, more professional success by remaining single!

Therefore, in the absence of extended family and community support, and in the absence of reasons (that is, significant social functions) for marriage, it must offer other advantages in order to remain an attractive competitive option.

In that regard, the authors believe that long-term commitments to other persons (as in marriage, pair-bonds, group marriages) offer satisfactions and advantages for most people that are difficult to get any other way. We don't mean the privilege of filing joint tax returns for the legally married, though that remains a real consideration so long as our tax structure is inequitable toward single people.

Perhaps we're just being old fashioned, but we find it nice to have a "Home Planet" shared with others over a long period of time. There are shared plans and anticipations, anniversaries, and, as we grow older, a richness of shared memories. Life, which is in so many ways disjointed, temporary, and centerless, can gain some continuity and coherence through marriage, or other pair-bond. However, there is a difference between advantage and necessity. Marriage continues to offer many advantages, in our view. But at the same time, if marriage has become economically, sexually, and socially unnecessary, it scarcely adds to its viability where it also takes away one's freedom to explore and enjoy additional relationships.

Therefore, we believe marriage becomes more attractive if it can be regarded as the first priority, the most important and enduring bond, but not necessarily the only significant love relationship. For those

whose additional needs are sexual, extramarital affairs would be viewed as supplemental to marriage: supporting it and sharing some of its intimacy functions, but not challenging its priority. This would be facilitated by means of dating after marriage and/or Compartment Four.

Such advantages are also possible in open marriage as described by the O'Neills. Those who choose such marriage styles can travel and can come home.

Not everyone will want outside sex. It certainly is not a must for the achievement of human happiness. We have interviewed many people whose sexually monogamous marriages continue to be fulfilling and exciting after many years.

But we see this as a matter of choice—not of necessity. And the evidence is clear that human beings indeed enjoy sexual variety and tend to become easily bored with one partner. This was pointed out by Kinsey and his colleagues, especially in their 1953 study, and more recently by Dr. Robert S. DeRopp, the author of *Sex Energy,* in 1969:

> The lamentations of the Micronesians, victims of interfering American administrators who put a stop to the long-established custom of elderly men taking young concubines, are also instructive:
>
> Older men often comment today that without young women to excite them and without the variety once provided by changing concubines, they have become sexually inadequate long before their time. To them, a wife is sexually exciting for only a few years after marriage.
>
> Nor is it only the human male who suffers from the emasculating effect of sexual boredom. Male monkeys that had wearied of their partners to the extent of being scarcely able to reach ejaculation perked up promptly and ejaculated speedily as soon as a different female was made available. Bulls, buffalo, sheep, and swine all show an enhancement of sexual performance when the number of females available to them is increased. The human male, in this respect, is no different from other mammals but, held in the fetters of monogamy, is frequently unable to obtain the sexual variety which his nature demands. Masters and Johnson emphasize that the maintenance of effective sexuality in the aging male depends on his level of sexual activity.

If desire for a variety of sexual partners is a quality of the human male, as indicated by DeRopp, it is also, as Kinsey found, a quality of the human female. However, in the past, the combination of social pressures from the community plus the need for a dependable source of income and a home in which to rear children prevented women from expressing this desire. The risk of pregnancy made responsible outside sex usually impossible unless one was pregnant, infertile, or past menopause.

Now, on the basis of research in physiology, endocrinology, and a number of other fields, Dr. Mary Jane Sherfey in her article, "The Evolution and Nature of Female Sexuality in Relation to Psychoanalytic Behavior," which appeared in the *Journal of the American Psychoanalytic Association* in 1966, has amassed a great deal of evidence that women may well have an insatiable sex drive, like the sex drive of certain female primates whose anatomy is much like ours:

> Having no cultural restrictions, these primate females will perform coitus from twenty to fifty times a day during the week of estrus, usually with several series of copulation in rapid succession.
> If necessary, they flirt, solicit, present and stimulate the male in order to obtain successive coitions.
> *They will "consort" with one male for several days until he is exhausted, then take up with another. . . .*
> I suggest that something akin to this behavior could be paralleled by the human female if her civilization allowed it.

Is civilization going to allow it? Hold on to your hats, men! Remember that the social and medical advances of this century have removed most of the blocks to the enjoyment of sexual variety by women. The result is that in some estimates close to half of all married women alive today in the United States have had one or more extramarital affairs. Not only that, but in our experience it is difficult to find a woman who does not at least fantasize a variety of sexual activities with a variety of partners.

Is it really necessary to repress such fantasies? Most of the catastrophic expectations about extramarital sex are, as we have shown, in large part irrational. This is not to say that its effects can never be unpleasant and, at times, destructive. By recognizing that outside sex is not necessarily all those awful things you were programmed to believe, an additional bonus arrives: psychological freedom to relate to others with an inner assurance that it needn't be terrible and catastrophic if that closeness brings sexual contact. For as we pointed out at the beginning of this chapter, the most crippling feature of the fear of outside sex is not that it inhibits sex and love per se, but that it indirectly inhibits many other activities and friendships that one imagines might lead to sex.

Finally we must resolve the mystery about the title of this chapter. It is simply that for millions of people, outside sex is still considered Public Enemy Number One—worse than risking death on the highway. How many married persons do you know who would rather risk death on the highway by driving home after too much to drink than call their spouses and announce that they are staying out all night? Everyone who drinks and drives does not get caught dead on the highway—but neither does everyone who stays out all night get caught in a destructive bed scene.

However, the dominant attitude of our society is well summed up in the report of a movie showing a sexy couple approaching a bedroom. You watch them beginning to undress; the audience becomes restless; the female is looking more and more seductive and the male is looking more and more aggressive. Suddenly his body is hovering over hers and gasps can be heard throughout the audience. Within seconds he has a nylon cord around her neck and she is dead. Gasps turn to sighs as more than one in the audience shows great relief: "Whew, I thought something *bad* was going to happen." For traditional audiences, it is clearly better to be dead than caught in bed.

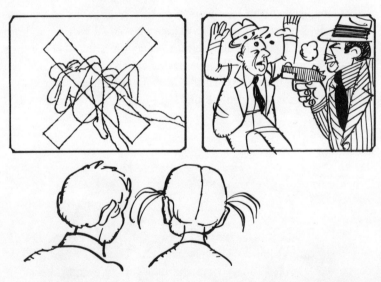

Our children can watch literally hundreds of killings a week, but never an adult taking a shower and going to bed nude—even alone! We vote to deprive sex of that much power. To compare the risk of coitus with the risk of death or the sight of coitus with the sight of death is to give sex inordinate power. We affirm that sex is not a matter of life and death. Better dead than caught in bed? No way!!

chapter 8

the case for multiple intimacies

We all understand what multiple means, but, indeed, what is "intimacy"? Some would say that at the moment of sexual climax one experiences maximum intimacy. We would disagree. You may have a glowing beautiful feeling that your loved one is close to you, and even sharing your ecstasy, but, in our view, fully experiencing your own orgasm focuses virtually all available attention on your own body and your own feelings, making intimacy with another person most unlikely. We believe the time both before and after orgasm to be far more conducive to true intimacy than the moments of orgasm itself. Although much is written about simultaneous orgasm, it is the awareness that your partner is experiencing ecstasy at the same time and the "bigness" of two orgasms at once that makes the event special—not what we would regard as an intimate exchange. However, when two partners climax separately, we believe it is quite possible for the non-climaxing partner to have a deep feeling of intimacy toward the climaxing partner.

Such one-sided intimacies are not rare. Often we feel very intimate with someone whose attention is focused on someone (something) else:

watching your spouse read to your three-year-old; listening to your daughter play the French horn, observing your mother withdraw to let the children settle it themselves . . . etc.

All of this makes "intimacy" harder and harder to define. But at least we can eliminate some common inaccuracies regarding sex, love, and intimacy. Often we hear speakers say: "Sex is intimate" or "Sex is the most intimate expression between two persons who deeply love each other" or "Sex is an expression of deep love." The implication is that *all* sex is intimate. The fact is that sex *may* or *may not* be intimate. It is our educated guess that the vast majority of sexual encounters occur without intimacy. Too often, especially in dealing with human sexuality, professionals state what they would *"like to be"* as what *"is."* What's more, they often become moralistic about "good sex" and "bad sex" according to their personal beliefs, with little regard as to whether or not the participants enjoyed a good time and caused no harm to anyone.

What is the relationship of intimacy to masturbation, prostitution, and casual sex? After all, none of these could have flourished all these centuries if "sex" were indeed restricted to an "intimate expression of a deep love between two persons." What kind of intimacy comes to mind when a sailor who has been on shipboard for three months has sex with a native woman with whom he has no commonality except a few moments of body language?

True, in every case of coitus there may be what we will describe as extraorbital intimacy, but we still have "glory holes" and the whole tea room scene* to explode the intimacy myth. A glory hole is a hole in the partitions between two stalls in a men's toilet. One man puts his penis through the hole and the other fondles or sucks it. Even the most imaginative could hardly call this intimate. Many married men indulge in this kind of "instant sex" with gays. Even though they are primarily heterosexual, they find this the least "involving" way to enjoy fellatio and relieve sexual tension. Our gay friends confirm the high percentage of married men seeking "blow jobs."

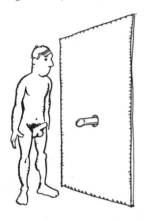

John and Sally have been married ten years. Since the birth of their first child eight years ago, Sally hasn't worked. They now have three children, and the second is in kindergarten.

John is a landscape architect. Last year they moved from their old but comfortable apartment in the city to a small redwood house that Sally designed and John landscaped. It overlooks the bay, and is a real joy to both of them.

In addition, they have a circle of mutual friends with whom they spend much of their spare time, and both of them are devoted parents to their three beautiful children. Not only that, but this marriage has another happy aspect: both in-laws have also become genuine friends.

*Tea room scene means sex activity in men's toilets, thus "T room."

John's folks think Sally is a very special person. And Sally's parents respect and admire John.

But despite the outward appearance of marital bliss, John and Sally do have problems. Sally describes herself as being very sensuous and sexual. Before their marriage, she had had several lovers and enjoyed a variety of sexual activities.

In addition to her lovers, Sally had a very close girl friend in whom she confided everything. "I could tell Lisa everything. There was just no shame at all between us," she recalls.

And Sally enjoyed her job as an architectural draftsman. It was through her job that she met John.

"He was, and is, a very handsome and sexy-looking guy," she says. "I was attracted to him immediately, and after a month we were talking marriage. We shared so many interests, and our backgrounds were so similar. When John didn't try to get me into bed on the first date, I realized that he was certainly different from the other men I had known. As a matter of fact, it turned out that the seducing was up to me, and it was a real challenge! John's lovemaking was inexperienced and certainly not what I'd been used to. However, he seemed to keep improving, and I was convinced that given enough time, I could turn any man into a satyr!"

Alas, it just wasn't to be. John's only driving interest was, and still is, landscape architecture. Although he developed into a good lover when the mood struck or when Sally was able to seduce him, there was a definite problem—their sexual appetites and preferences were not compatible. Sally liked vigorous sex in a variety of positions. John liked tender one position sex. Sally liked oral sex. John did not.

In addition, John was somewhat "emotionally closed up," to use Sally's description. He very seldom shared his inner feelings of sadness or anger or joy. As a close friend, he compared poorly with Sally's friend, Lisa.

Despite this, Sally truly respects her husband as a person and as a fellow professional. Despite her unconventional sex history, she is traditional in that she is proud to be his wife and the mother of his children. In addition, he often shares his professional problems with her as a colleague. He values her advice, and when he is very busy, he often asks Sally to prepare drawings for him.

Therefore, when Sally's mind occasionally turns to divorce, she is immediately confronted with a long list of tangible advantages of her marriage.

1. *Pleasant comfortable life.* The single most important point is that her life is comfortable with John. He is pleasant to be with. There are very few active negatives, just a few deficiencies—not enough sparkle, openness, or sex. Then come the material, practical advantages . . .
2. *The three children.* A divorce would disrupt their current pleasant family situation.
3. *The redwood house overlooking the bay.* It isn't especially large but Sally really loves it. Since the house also doubles as John's studio, and the yard is his plant nursery, it would be more practical for him to keep the house.
4. *John is a great father.* He is truly marvelous with the children. He is the kind of relaxed, low-key individual who never minds having the kids around when he's working. Thus, since the studio is at home, he often baby-sits, which gives Sally considerable free time for her own interests.
5. *Their circle of friends.* Sally has watched other couples go through divorce, and is aware that their friends usually take sides and often lose interest in them as single people. Their suburban life is definitely couple-oriented. One invites Sally and John as a couple, but seldom are unattached men and women invited.
6. *Their in-laws are their friends.* Both John's and Sally's parents live close by and they truly enjoy their family visits.

For these and other reasons, there is a great deal at stake in John and Sally's maintaining their marriage, as there is in many marriages. This is perhaps why marriage is one of the most difficult relationships in which to be consistently truthful. It is too risky and often there is far too much to lose.

Obviously, this type of accounting still doesn't prevent an ever-increasing number from seeking divorce. Widespread affluence makes things possible now that few could have afforded or indulged in a century ago. Nevertheless we stick to our point: truthfulness tends to decrease as the stakes go up.

In this chapter, we have used the words "honest" and "truthful" somewhat interchangeably. "Truthful" is the more accurate word, however, for it implies greater correspondence with reality. On a brief out of town trip, Sally had a super sex experience. It was great to really play again and enjoy many different positions and, wow!, the oral sex really turned her on. She took delight in both giving and receiving. Sally is one of those persons who can experience instant intimacy. She feels very intimate during nude sex play. She enjoys showering together, oil massage, etc. She has learned to love and let go. Her out of town experience is the kind of event that advocates of open marriage say should be shared with the spouse. However, Sally has good reason to believe that John is in fact a very jealous person. His feelings about extramarital sex are that it is unthinkable, intolerable, immoral, catastrophic. And Sally feels she has too much to lose to be honest with John.

Sally, like many of us, entered into marriage accepting the honesty demands inherent in the ideal marriage, traditional or open. At the time of her marriage, she intended to speak the truth fully to John about all matters. She did not foresee circumstances in which this might conflict with important personal desires. She expected that, after a few months of living together, he would respond to her charm and become a more warm and open person. She also expected that his sexual desires would more nearly equal her own. You see, when the children were very small and they had less money, Sally was extremely busy and usually physically tired. She thought that her need for wild sex was over. She enjoyed John's soft tender sex and fully anticipated that should her old desires return, John would meet the challenge. But despite goodwill on her part and marriage counseling, it didn't happen. She is now presented with a real conflict. Sharing her fantasies of exciting sex with licking and sucking would be unthinkable. Sharing her frustration would be cruel. Already she must withhold the truth about feelings. She has several options regarding behavior. We will present only four.

1. *Exercise self-discipline to avoid any more outside sex.* The risk is that her lack of sexual fulfillment might backfire if, as a result, she became resentful of the marriage and increasingly critical of John. And what about honesty? Should she tell John about her frustration—which is real? Should she tell him about her opportunities for affairs and how noble she is in turning them down? Sally actually has two needs. One is for intimate sharing such as she had with her close friend before marriage, and the other is for sex.

2. *Continue with outside sex as needed, and describe it rather frankly to John.* This would fulfill the honesty requirement. However, as we said, he is a jealous sort who is likely to blow his lid. The risk is that such confrontation might cause irreparable damage to a basically comfortable marital relationship.

3. *Inform John of her desire and need for Compartment Four.* She would then encourage him to adopt such a private compartment for himself.

    a. If John's response is neutral, then this third choice becomes a declared, but unilateral, Compartment Four. That is, Sally has informed John of her intentions but there is no mutual agreement to include Compartment Four as part of the structure of the marriage.

    b. If John agrees, then the choice is easy and clear: a Compartment Four marriage.

    c. If John disagrees and protests, then Sally is left with choices 1, 2, or 4.

4. *Have outside sex and exercise discretion.* This is an undeclared, unilateral Compartment Four. One spouse decides that for her, or his, feeling of self-worth, she or he must act in a certain way. To act otherwise would be untrue to oneself and one's self-concept. Remember that Compartment Four retains responsibility and conscience. One decides on the privacy of Compartment Four when the acts themselves would not truly harm anyone, but knowledge of the activities might evoke an irrational, but nonetheless real, negative response.

For too long, society has automatically taken the side of the spouse who follows the letter of the law, even though such compliance has caused great hostility, frustration, and suffering. Quiet desperation is socially well-accepted. The problem is to distinguish between inconsiderate self-indulgence and assertion of one's own needs with consideration of others. Can anyone do that for anyone else? Who should decide what's right for Sally, except Sally? Should John decide for Sally? Should the Social Action Committee of the synagogue or church? Should the PTA? The neighbors? The obscenity laws? Whose right is it to decide?

Sally based her decision on what she believed would be best for her, her husband, and the marriage. The truth is that she is a highly sexual person and also has a great capacity for openness as well as a tendency to become sad or bitchy after depriving herself of outlets. Her repressed needs and subsequent behavior would not be at all good for her husband, children, the marriage, or herself. The first option was quickly eliminated.

In the second, it was John's nature that determined her decision. Sally was fully capable of having affairs and speaking frankly about them to John. When she fantasized the possibility of John's having an affair and telling her about it, she said her reaction would be more of fascination and curiosity, not jealousy. In fact, she said that she'd be overjoyed to see him taking a greater interest in sex. But John is uncommunicative and jealous and his probable reaction to news of Sally's affair ruled out option number two.

Sally preferred the third possibility, establishing a private compartment, hopefully with John's consent. But although she brought up the subject with him several times, he seemed uninterested (perhaps a cover for his feeling threatened), and changed the subject.

Therefore, by the process of elimination, Sally established her own Compartment Four and continued to enjoy outside sex with discretion. She decided to act and judge situations on her own and to exercise caution in deciding what not to tell.

We are aware that there are other approaches to this couple's problems, all the way from divorce to marriage counseling and sex clinics. Divorce was not the solution for Sally and John. As we stated, they did try counseling and John saw no reason to visit a sex clinic. Sally never told him about the increase in her frustration that occurred with her increased free time.

There are many women and men in Sally's predicament. When presented with totally unexpected, difficult choices, they may often find themselves doing something that they never would have believed possible. A person who has been compulsively truthful up to this point may discover that discretion is both necessary and kind. This separateness may have hundreds of different origins. We are concerned not just with Sally's, but also with situations where one partner feels a deep conflict over a potentially serious relationship desperately needed for personal growth and happiness. Too often sharing this conflict with the spouse would be disastrous. We find that such outside relationships are often sacrificed to maintain the image of togetherness, not to maintain honesty, since the fantasy and frustration are not shared!

At the point where the conflict is recognized, the status quo is gone. Change has already taken place. A common way to deal with the change is to keep the conflict a secret and work toward not recognizing what you do in fact recognize. In other words, many spouses bury the temptation as though it had never happened. Their guts may be churning inside but they endure.

These choices are difficult ones to make. To resist a potentially growthful and fulfilling relationship is cruelty directed toward oneself. On the other hand, what do we do when honesty will almost surely result in cruelty to another? Our conclusion is that real honesty must be primarily with oneself and toward one's own motives. If you are honestly sacrificing candor out of love for someone, that is quite different from doing so merely to preserve your own image.

For years and years such complexities have been brushed aside while candor about all important matters has been regarded as a requisite for a good marriage. There are exceptions, however, which are accepted by almost everyone. For example, as we have noted, withholding the truth about frustration, anger, and fantasies is quite common even in so-called honest marriages. It is considered far more deceitful to withhold information about a relatively insignificant physical act than it is to withhold deeply significant feelings, but once anything is withheld, the principle of privacy and consideration for the feelings of others is already established. Indeed, it is our belief that few marriages could survive without selective honesty. But we do not believe that it is any more dishonest to conceal private activities than it is to withhold strong negative emotions. In fact, marriages which allow private activities for each spouse help to reduce negative emotions, especially feelings of being trapped.

As the case of Sally and John has indicated, whenever there is a vested interest in a relationship, one cannot always afford to be totally honest. But in marriage, this fact is painful to accept because you thought you had chosen this person because you felt you could share everything. The conflict arises when your fantasies and desires are not easily shared, and the conflict greatly increases when the possibility of acting-out a fantasy is considered.

Throughout this book, we have emphasized that personal growth and fulfillment often involve hobbies, sports, job changes, travel, and so on. In each of these, there may be varying degrees of restriction depending on the circumstances and attitudes of those involved. We have repeatedly referred to outside sex as a source of growth simply because it is the most difficult one for people to handle. Outside romantic or sexual relationships have received maximum restriction and disapproval along with a minimum of serious consideration. So many people automatically accept the "wrongness" of extramarital sex that serious and intelligent discussion is excluded and we don't learn much about it as a resource. This inability to take an honest and open look at the matter was stated as early as 1921 by James Harvey Robinson, author of *The Mind in the Making:*

> If a thing is held to be sacred, it is the center of what may be called a defense complex, and a reasonable consideration of the merits of the case will not be tolerated. When an issue is declared a "moral" one ... an emotional state is implied which makes reasonable compromise and adjustment impossible, for "moral" is a word on somewhat the same plane as "sacred," and has much the same qualities and similar effects on our thinking. In dealing with the relations of the sexes, the terms "pure" and "impure" introduce mystic and irrational moods alien to clear analysis and reasonable adjustments.

It is thus that we have attempted to examine the relationship between truthfulness and marriage, and seriously consider outside sex as a possible option for personal growth and fulfillment.

The traditional message has been that sexual monogamy and honesty are sacred, hence not open to truthful evaluation. Had J. H. Robinson lived in more recent times, he would have had to contend with a new wave of obscurantist terminology—that of theologians who intone "If sex is not an expression of an I-Thou relationship . . ." and of some psychiatrists who claim that outside sex is always symptomatic of character neurosis. The words change, but the meaning stays the same: Don't evaluate it—just label it!

In the same way, one still occasionally hears the message that all intimacies outside of marriage must be suspected of uncontrollable passion with resulting irresponsibility. Our case histories deny that evaluation.

And the jealous spouse is still supported in his or her righteous fury when a partner desires outside intimacy and/or sex!

These messages are both unbelievably strong and unbelievably irrational, whether couched in old-fashioned or psychiatric jargon. In terms of personal growth, the price of following these messages is appalling: "Because I am married, I must not learn about people, or about life, or about sex through any outside activities. Intimacy and sex are not legitimate sources of growth and understanding of the human predicament, except within marriage. Extramarital relationships are plots of the devil to destroy all that is sacred and good."

For years the public has been bombarded with images associating outside intimacy and sex with irresponsibility. There are enough such cases to keep a successful campaign going for years. What needs to be said is that whereas all that is true, there is another side to it. Millions of responsible people do, in fact, use extramarital intimacy and sex to achieve personal growth.

To return for a moment to our friend Sally, you will recall that she chose to have outside sex and exercise discretion. But she still has another decision to make. Will she think of herself as cheating or will she join the underground?

Cheating is when you feel that what you are doing is wrong, but you want to do it badly enough to carry the guilt, or the compulsion is so strong that you cannot help yourself.

Going underground means that you believe what you are doing is right, but the occupation army (societal institutions) has power over your job, custody of your children, and carries the future opportunity to prevent your earning a living and living with dignity, but most of all, it has power over your marriage.

Persons who join the underground believe that their lifestyles are best for them, even though unacceptable to the larger community and, often, to their spouses. Millions of gay and bisexual persons are in the underground. They are not ashamed of their sexual orientation. They simply must keep their behavior secret or suffer severe consequences. With them are hundreds of thousands of persons enjoying outside sexual relationships about which they feel good. They are responsible persons who are highly motivated not to cause harm or hurt, and to exercise discretion.

To date, there is little choice for people like Sally, who is much more imaginative and outgoing than her spouse. One must deny personal fulfillment, cheat, or else join the underground. We think of Sally as belonging to the underground. We hope she thinks that way of herself.

If the concept of a private compartment in marriage were accepted, there would be a built-in escape valve, an opportunity for the conscientious withholding of selected information without breaking any rules. It is a matter of making the rules fit human needs, instead of trying to fit human needs into rules already proved inadequate and obsolete.

An additional insight into the relationship between marriage and truthfulness in our culture is given by George Bach and Ronald Deutsch in their book entitled *Pairing*.

> Ours is a family-oriented culture. And it so values family life that it treats unmarried adults at best as undeveloped, immature, and incomplete—and at worst as failures and willful renegades who cannot or will not take up a respectable and responsible family role.
>
> The insidious result is that—while giving lip service to the overriding importance of love—the vast majority of Americans actually make marriage status the real goal of male-female relationships. The chance for love disappears, as we shall see, as men and women try to distort their perceptions of the other, of themselves, and of the relationship into good marriage bets. They dare not risk being authentic: it might spoil the sunny dream of rising out of tacit disgrace.

We would add that for the many who are already married, divorce is threatening for the same reason. You would be thrown right into the group of cultural rejects—the unmarried.

Thus, the vested interest in marriage also includes the status of marriage which, although no longer *necessary,* still retains many social and economic advantages. So let us admit that many persons have a great deal at stake when they continue to maintain a marriage that is sorely lacking in one or more qualities such as warmth, excitement, joy, and intimacy. At this point in her life, Sally's particular need was for much more sex and openness than her marriage could provide. Her marriage was sexually and emotionally lukewarm at best, but offered other advantages, so she joined the sexual underground by establishing a unilateral Compartment Four.

Others in similar situations look for intimacy in psychotherapy or T-groups of various kinds. Some are inexpensive. But if not, expense can be a real problem. Not only that, but away from the T-group or therapist's office, many persons still experience great difficulties in trying to establish satisfying relationships. Their difficulty is not so much in talking to someone, it's a matter of feeling some essential involvement with them. Because what remains after talking is the same longing, the same aloneness, the same words left unspoken. What a feeling of helplessness, to have gone through all the motions of communication, and still to have failed.

Can this helplessness be overcome?

Not always. Not all of us are like Sally—outgoing, attractive, young, and with new contacts easily made. But many others don't quite know how to reach out for outside relationships. Others feel that age and similar factors are against them. It's hard to forget the young girl who wrote to Miss Lonelyhearts that she was a good dancer and so on, and wanted to go out with boys, but she had no nose. We hope we have not created existential despair in some by presenting desirable relationships as always easy to come by. We admit that, for many, it takes a very special kind of guts to reach out. Some can accept playing golf with a handicap yet still enjoy playing. And despite our praise of human relationships as a source of growth and fulfillment, we know there are other ways, and that life can still be meaningful.

For those in cold marriages or with no significant relationships, we suggest reading *Pairing,* in which Bach and Deutsch describe methods for achieving intimacy quickly with strangers. We are sure that their approach works for many. To put it more accurately, it isn't the technique that works—*you* do! What we are suggesting is that what they call pairing methods can be used to create intimate relationships to supplement nonintimate marriages, when there are strong reasons other than intimacy to continue the marriage. They describe intimacy as:

A relationship characterized by the transparency, authenticity, and immediacy of interaction of the partners, in which each permits the other the experience and expression of his feelings; thus, essentially, a relationship of trust and sharing, without fear of dealing openly with conflict.

We would add, however, that achieving intimacy, like so many kinds of human relationships, is anything but simple. Sometimes the essence of what is intimate depends on an individual's depth, intensity, and transparency. But sometimes intimacy is quite the opposite; years and years of trusted friendship make you feel intimate with someone with whom you do not in fact share secrets. With this sort of friend, an important secret could be shared, whereas a series of other secrets may be withheld out of deference to the values of a long-time friend.

We have chosen to describe four types of intimacy. This division is arbitrary—there may actually be only two or as many as eight or more. We just happen to find four types relevant to our theme. They are not mutually exclusive and two or more may occur in the same relationship, but, in our view, one type tends to dominate.

1. *Extraorbital Intimacy:* This is best described as intimate relationships that do not exert pressures on your everyday functioning. Extraorbital intimacy ranges from the telling-all to a bartender to ongoing meetings with persons with whom you feel immediately close but whose friendship does not place undue demands on your time or energy.

For example, instant intimacy is often easy when sitting next to a congenial person in an airplane. How easy to be honest and admit how angry your children make you, or how your wife irritates you, when you know you will never have to meet this person again.

At the other end of the spectrum of extraorbital intimacies are those warm, tender relationships that do not occupy much of your time, but whenever you get together, you are intimate with each other without a second's lead time. Such extraorbital intimacies are especially beautiful because the cost-benefit ratio is so favorable to both of you. Each brings to the meeting an expectation of joy at being together, leaving many of the practical problems of your everyday orbits behind.

Intelligent and sensitive persons are aware that extraorbital intimacies are usually escapes. You are keenly aware that the uniqueness of the relationship depends on the situation that allows two persons to relate joyfully within a kind of vacuum.

Extraorbital intimates may see each other only once, or maybe once in five or six years. They are very intimate and open with each other when they meet, and if several years later they happen to be in the vicinity, they will call. But if not, there may be a letter or telephone call. The number of extraorbital intimacies is almost limitless.

2. *Enduring Intimacy:* This is quite the opposite from the above. The intimate aspects of the relationship evolve through years of trust and mutual respect, and rely on having so many shared experiences. With a few exceptions, almost any important information may be related to an enduring intimate. But if part of your lifestyle definitely offends your enduring intimate, you would only relate it if you were desperate, needed help, or were willing to pay the price of offending someone near and dear to you.

The experience of enduring intimacy often makes you feel good and warm all over. Chances are that you can share almost everything in confidence.

3. *Romantic Intimacy:* Here, the desire to please the other person and to be loved in return takes priority. Of course, you want desperately to be yourself. You want him or her to love the real you. Nevertheless, the promise of romance often motivates one to suddenly feel and act differently, to develop a sudden taste for the checked shirts and wide ties she likes. Why not? In romantic intimacy, the tendency is to put one's best foot forward. Here, it is the feeling of being in love that comes first, and honesty may be stretched quite a bit to create the romantic image and atmosphere.

For example, Victor says, "Mary, it's okay if you can't reschedule the concert on Friday, we can go to the Rockies some other time. Stop worrying, honey, let's go take a walk together and maybe stop at The Cheese Palace for one of those plates filled with all kinds of cheese. Okay?" In reality, Victor is terribly disappointed. The vacation plans had coincided with the date their best friends would be at the resort in Colorado and he especially wanted to be with them. What benefit is there in being honest? For example, Victor could have said, "Dammit, Mary, you and your career, sometimes I . . ." Certainly these thoughts are honest. Actually, Victor is devoted to Mary and is in fact more than willing to put up with the inconveniences. Obviously, Mary understands that Victor is in fact disappointed. The question is, What purpose is served by being honest and giving in to strong, fleeting flashes of anger and hostility?

Here is another example. When Tom was courting Mary, she was an ardent toboggan fan. Every spare moment, she was off to the hills. Since Tom didn't join her very often, it was clear that this was not his favorite sport. But once in a while on weekends he would go along with her and pretend to enjoy it. Actually, he liked snow, loved being with Mary, but was petrified each time the toboggan left the top of the hill. Later in the relationship he told her of his fear. But at first, it was more important to the progress of their romance to be a fun, cooperative person open to new experiences than to reveal himself as a scaredy-cat, afraid of toboggan rides.

Blunt honesty may often be avoided to maintain the romantic aspects of a relationship. "Ugh, that dress looks horrible!" is hardly a way to start a date. Much better and also true to say, "It's so great to be with you—I'm really looking forward to our day together."

Lovers especially do not care about being absolutely truthful about all their weaknesses. In fact, pretending not to have a weakness may be the very best way to help overcome it—like whistling in the dark! We believe that it is often beneficial to go soft on some weaknesses without, however, giving the opposite impression.

4.   *Honesty Intimacy:* The fourth type of intimacy is unlike that with a stranger or bartender, an old friend, or a lover. Here, those involved have arbitrarily made honesty their top priority. This is not just simple here-and-now intimacy, but a commitment that the next time, and forever thereafter, there will be complete honesty.

This can include hurting an intimate for the sake of candor. It means negating some of the social niceties. It usually requires integrating into a sophisticated lifesytle the naive, often blunt openness of a child. The relationship may or may not be filled with romantic inclinations. Year after year, this kind of relationship becomes similar to enduring intimacy. But when it comes to put up or shut up, honesty takes priority. This radical type of honesty is discussed further in regard to a relationship we call super-friendship.

Although there are clear overlaps it is our impression that one of the four types of intimacy tends to prevail.

Traditional marriage appears to combine the last three. We are certainly aware of the fact that romantic and enduring intimacy often go together in marriage. But when one partner is far more romantic than the other, the need to preserve the enduring aspect of the marriage may make honesty well nigh impossible. If one partner definitely feels less in love than the other, but still tender and affectionate, should he or she confess that they now have a one-sided relationship? Should one say, "Darling, I don't love you as much as I think you love me, but I do appreciate you and I'm glad we enjoy so many things together. Can you possibly understand that you just don't turn me on anymore? I can respond to you, and certainly enjoy that. But it sure isn't like our relationship fifteen years ago! It's just that your turn-on outlived mine, dear. Don't you feel better now that I've leveled with you? What if I had been dishonest and made a tiny effort to pretend our feelings were a bit more equal? Wouldn't that have spoiled everything? Honesty between marriage partners is always best, right?" Wrong. But it is always best with a super-friend. Super-friend is a new term. It is a person with whom you have honesty intimacy, defined earlier.

We have already observed that power and honesty make poor bedfellows. Hence it should not be a surprise that we recommend that super-friends be sought among those who have no power over your life. Except in unusual instances that requirement generally excludes bosses, who might fire you, rich aunts, who might disinherit you, and so on. And if you don't already have a super-friend, a good place to start looking, as Bach and Deutsch suggest, is anywhere: at the laundromat, on the bus, in the supermarket. For where to go after you say hello, we refer you to *Pairing*.

Super-friendship includes, by definition, qualities like transparency, authenticity, and sharing of feelings from center to center. This separates super-friendship from ordinary friendship which may be based on mutual interests, like stamps or tennis, with little self-revelation.

In addition, power and vulnerability dimensions are almost wholly absent from a super-friendship. No mortgage is shared, no children are being reared jointly, and if the friendship ends, you may feel a deep loss—but no lawyers are needed, no jobs are threatened, no alimony will be collected, no children will be taken away.

Now, what is so special about super-friendship? Have you ever felt so exuberantly proud of yourself that you wanted to burst into the room with childlike freedom and brag about the greatness within you? But you wouldn't want to sound that conceited even to a good friend, so you modify your feelings of exuberance and modestly say, "Things went very well."

But a super-friend would rejoice in your freedom of expression.

A super-friend accepts you and your feelings, unencumbered with the usual social limitations.

The phone rings. "Hello, what's up?" A super-friend would feel free to answer, "Could you call back? I'm fucking."

With a super-friend, you do not have to tell everything, but you are able to. A super-friend will not intentionally hold back meaningful information and is encouraged to speak with total freedom. To say "I'm busy" would elicit a mild feeling of curiosity, whereas "I'm fucking" is not only accurate but produces a feeling of warmth and pleasure.

Super-friendship also provides the opportunity to express negative feelings honestly. "I'm lonely as hell. I need to be touched, to be held close, to be loved. I feel miserable."

Like an ethical psychiatrist, a super-friend will not use your confidence to betray you. Information learned goes into a special super-friend compartment and receives the total respect it deserves.

Of course, it may be easier and less threatening to fragment our revelations. We may share one corner of our feelings with one person, and a different corner with another person, but remain secure by not removing all barriers with anyone. With one, you discuss sex, but not finances. With another, you discuss religion, but you don't describe your hostility toward your children. With a third, you are honest about your feelings toward the children, but never discuss sex. None of these are super-friendships.

There seems to be a built-in protection against letting one person know everything about you. But to share your whole inner circle of feelings—deepest fears, wildest yearnings, hostilities, fantasies of greatness—this is rare! And this is super-friendship.

Super-friendship demands psychological nakedness. You stand bare and unashamed and proud of your new power to combat inner loneliness.

Nonentanglement in each other's daily struggles is an advantage for super-friends. Social circles and interests may overlap somewhat, but in order to avoid the power contaminant, it is important that each super-friend has friends and interests that extend well beyond the relationship. For when one friend begins to depend too much on the friendship for his or her emotional gratification, the super-friendship is in danger. As dependency goes up, honesty tends to decrease because of fear of possible loss. By maintaining separate lives, super-friends are able to maintain a healthy perspective and at the same time be deeply involved in each other as human beings.

It is important to understand this. Super-friendship is primarily supportive and therefore nonthreatening to other relationships. This is one reason why super-friends can seldom be romantic lovers. As soon as romance enters the picture, complete honesty tends to bow out. Romance is enhanced by a sprinkling of mystery—incense, candlelight, and wine. And the desire to please and remain fascinating and intriguing to a lover tends to exclude the kind of blunt honesty demanded of a super-friend. For super-friends can be rough on each other! They are truthful at the expense of being less lovable. What a sure way to destroy romance!

We recognize the need for both: the need to bare our weaknesses and yearnings and anger without fear of rejection, and the need to project our desirable sides to enjoy the passions of love and romance. And there is a third need: for the kind of ongoing relationship marriage can be, though it may be neither as open as super-friendship nor retain all its romantic love throughout the years.

Most people need all three. Yet the most intimate of the three may not be sexual at all. The most sexual may not be the most enduring. The most enduring will probably not be the most romantic. And the most romantic is rarely the most honest.

Super-friendship represents, in a sense, an underground movement. We who are truly honest with another person recognize our vulnerability. But we have pride in our friendships, and a feeling of relief at being able to share weaknesses. We realize that many of those not in the underground could not tolerate the kinds of truths exchanged between super-friends. Would a doctor's patients want to know that he is afraid of surgery? Therefore, we realize that public exposure of the truths shared by super-friends might destroy our marriages, our jobs, our social acceptance, and make life miserable for our children. But for those who meet the challenge of relating honestly to a super-friend, this is experienced as an exciting landmark on the road to personal identity, a refreshing kind of purity that is almost impossible to find otherwise.

Again, marriage can rarely be such a pure relationship. It is an inherently complex institution involving a home, often children, and usually a sharing of life's everyday problems. The joy of maintaining both romance and honesty with one and the same person over the years only occasionally overcomes the compromises inherent in the situation.

We have used a degree of license in describing the honesty between super-friends as complete and total. We do not claim that it is absolute. But relative to any other relationships we have known, the degree of honesty is so great that we found such superlatives irresistible. We do recognize binds regarding confidences. For instance, a super-friend's sister comes up and says, "I'm pregnant—but don't tell my brother no matter what." Such binds seldom occur. But when they do, one can say, "Yes, she told me something in confidence. Sorry, I am just not free to repeat it." A super-friend would accept this explanation with a real sense of respect.

If super-friends are so honest, open, and intimate, just what is the relationship between a super-friendship and sex? Super-friendship cannot be based on sexual attraction with honesty second, or on romance with honesty second. For then the relationship becomes a love affair, in which each participant hesitates to be honest if the love-relationship will be threatened by it. Each is involved in pleasing the other and hesitates to risk turn-offs. Also, both with lovers and marriage partners, there is the cloud of potential jealousy hovering overhead. Jealousy cannot be a part of super-friendship. Each super-friend has her or his own life. Super-friends freely discuss each other's loves, lovers, frustrations, victories, defeats, strengths, and weaknesses. We know of super-friendships that have included occasional, limited sex. Super-friends stand "bare and unashamed," and can do so literally as well as figuratively. Limited sex means that sex is possible as a matter of curiosity or to symbolically eliminate all barriers, but is not primary.

To be even more specific, the following are examples of how super-friends may deal with sex:

Case 1: Jane was always sexually attracted to Jim, but Jim saw her as a confidante and preferred to exclude explicit sex. He enjoyed expressing his feelings about his loves and sexual partners to her. Jane made it clear that the attraction was there, and at the same time accepted the relationship without sex. Jim explained further that the super-friend relationship was terribly important to him and that, because of his past experiences with affairs, he felt that their super-friendship would be threatened if they had intercourse.

Case 2: John was very much attracted to Mary, but Mary was single and John was married. Mary had had several affairs, some quite rewarding and all involving a living-together arrangement. John and Mary had coitus twice, but Mary did not want to continue. Her super-friendship with John was a big slice of her emotional pie and she did not want to give any more to a man who had so many other commitments. She feared a one-sided romance. She wanted to keep the super-friend relationship as a long-range support and keep herself available for a separate sexual partner who could offer more of his time and energy and perhaps even marriage.

Case 3: George and Jean's relationship started out as an affair and developed into a super-friendship. After the romantic element diminished, they had sexual intercourse only rarely, but often met over a cup of coffee or a drink and enjoyed regular telephone super-friend type conversations.

Case 4: Linda was curious about trying sex with a woman and simply asked her super-friend Doris if she wanted to experiment. Doris was totally turned off by the idea. Linda later reported to Doris her success with another woman.

Case 5: With Amy and Bob, it was easy. Amy was heterosexual and Bob was strictly homosexual. They had no problems with honesty or activity.

To summarize, one must have an honest exchange regardless of sex and romance. It is possible to include sex within a super-friendship, but the tendency is to drift either toward romance or away from sex.

We recognize that many people do not have the need or desire for the kind of radical intimacy that is experienced in super-friendship. And some marriages are so intrinsically satisfying that additional close relationships do not seem necessary. However, we think the case can be made that, for many of us, a pattern of multiple intimacies offers a more rewarding lifestyle. Since extraorbital intimacy, romance, honesty, and enduring intimacy emphasize different characteristics, at least three or four relationships may be needed to experience all these dimensions at their fullest.

Having made what we feel is a strong case for multiple intimacies, we feel the need to add one more thought. Sometimes multiple intimacies mean no intimacies. In other words, you can spread yourself too thin. Or, by being involved with too many people, you might avoid being truly intimate with any of them.

Bach and Deutsch speak about this situation in *Pairing*. It is important to remember that their remarks are addressed to the possibility of transparency, openness, and so on which we call honesty intimacy. Nevertheless, we find what they have to say valuable in terms of our multiple-intimacies concept:

QUESTION:

For some reason I'm not sure I understand, I seem to keep falling in love with two men at the same time. I think I have real intimacy with both just now. One of them agrees. The other says this idea is impossible, that I must be shallow. Many of my friends are very critical; some even imply that I am promiscuous. Can I pair authentically with more than one person?

DR. BACH:

Authentic multiple pairing is possible, but extremely ambitious and energy-demanding, with a high risk of complicating love until it becomes chaotic and eventually superficial. The ability to pair-multiply is rare, but it may be checked out with the following test:

1. Can you sustain more than one sexual relationship, with satisfaction for both yourself and the respective partners?
2. Does a second sexual relationship provide carryover stimulation for the first, and vice versa, enhancing both relationships —not diminishing either of them?
3. Can you free yourself and your partners from jealousy, competitive comparisons, and possessiveness?
4. Is it stimulating—and not confusing—to have different aspects of your personality drawn into play for each partner?
5. Can you openly assert your preference for multiple pairing with both partners, without guilt or deception, without becoming a multiple cheat?
6. Are you sure you are not using multiple pairing to dilute each involvement and thus evade any true intimacy?
7. Are you sure you are not confusing multiple pairing with a more primitive desire for sexual variety?
8. Do you have the time, money, energy, planning skills, and independence of social approval to manage the inherent complexities of multiple relationships?

Unless you can honestly answer six of these eight questions with a genuine and unqualified *yes,* we recommend that you reconsider your interest in multiple pairing. However, if you can respond affirmatively there is nothing in our pairing principles that stands in the way of achieving multiple intimacy.

Thus, there is a limit to the total number of close relationships one can handle with positive benefit to all concerned. The limit depends on the individual. However, we find that it is possible to have an almost unlimited number of temporary extraorbital intimacies, since they do not, by definition, encroach on other commitments.

But even with regard to nontemporary relationships, we know several people who can answer six or even seven of Bach's questions with an unqualified yes. Some of them find his term "multiple cheat" objectionable. But we suspect he meant it as we would, namely, interfering with other obligations. With multiple intimacies, it requires a careful effort to see that no one is short-changed. Regarding sex, most people at least fantasize the need for sexual variety. We suggest that extraorbital sex, as one form of extraorbital intimacy, may often satisfy needs without disrupting households. Here we want to emphasize that the main factor that makes these nonmarital intimacies responsible is that both parties understand the contract. Too often, multiple intimacies are condemned not because of the principle of more than one intimacy, but because of the belief that one party is inevitably exploited. Our case histories disprove this.

And so we return to discretion, both in the sense of caution and of its dictionary definition as freedom to act or judge on one's own—the right to decide for oneself. This is the meaning of Compartment Four, the private compartment in a liberated marriage. Compartment Four is not the answer for everyone. But for many, it can provide a way to be married and still be you.

One person, married for more than twenty-five years, writes to us:

I feel toward my spouse as I do toward my parents.
I appreciate what they have done to help me be what I am.
I care for them. I want them to live full and happy lives.
I would sacrifice much for their well-being.
I do not enjoy being with them for long periods of time.
I enjoy visiting them because I care for them and want to con-

tribute toward their happiness. It is an indirect enjoyment now, rather than a direct one.

I feel with regard to my wife, that she has done a good job of rearing our children, from whom she and I derive a good deal of pleasure.

I enjoy taking her to social occasions, and on those rare occasions when we still make love, I enjoy it.

The moments when we share our memories are precious to us.

I also need novelty and excitement to make life worth living.

I have great potential for being bright-eyed and responsive and passionate. Should I let this die from disuse, and add myself to the numbers of defeated and dulled persons in our world?

I remain stubbornly unwilling to sacrifice my appreciation for my parents, my enjoyment of many aspects of life with my wife (including respect and loyalty), *or* the other activities and people which keep alive my bright-eyed and passionate side.

I do not find them mutually exclusive.

Rather, I find them complementing and strengthening each other.

Another writes:

My husband and I have a beautiful marriage.

We love doing things together.

We love just being together.

We love making love together.

But I also make love to others.

I do not know if he does or not.

We both have strong desires for autonomy and self-determination.

Although our marriage is our primary relationship, we regard each other as individuals not beholden to each other's whims when we are apart.

We deplore parent-child communications between spouses, each "allowing" some privilege or other.

Rather, as peers we agree to a degree of freedom and privacy without destroying our love, our intimacy, our marriage and indeed enhancing our respect, our autonomy, and our selfhood.

The case for multiple intimacies—and autonomy—has been made. We appreciate those people who prefer single intimacies. But at the same time, our goal is to crush forever the feeling of failure for those who cannot thrive on a single intimacy and to offer multiple intimacies as an alternate lifestyle.

Be together, but let there be spaces in your togetherness. And may the winds of the heavens dance around you!

Definitions and comments

ADDED-DIMENSION DATING: One-to-one relationships between opposite numbers in a couple-couple friendship. For example, consider the relationship between two heterosexual pairs: Alan and Sarah and Mike and Lorna. Added-dimension dating gives Alan and Lorna the opportunity to relate on a one-to-one basis, and for Sarah and Mike to do the same. This is an added dimension to the usual pattern in which they see each other as couples, and in which although the boys may do things together, and so may the girls, seldom does the female of one couple have the opportunity to become a close personal friend to the male of the other couple. Added-dimension dating makes this possible.

CHEATING: Cheating is when you feel that what you are doing is wrong, but you want to do it enough to carry the guilt, or the compulsion is so strong that you feel you cannot help yourself.

CONVENTIONAL MARRIAGE: A legal pair-bond between a male

and a female sanctioned by the state. Outside romantic and/or sexual relationships are excluded, and the marriage partners are expected to display possessive jealousy whenever a breach of conventions is known to have occurred.

DATING AFTER MARRIAGE: An arrangement whereby married persons meet persons other than their spouses to enjoy a private togetherness without worrying about a third party. To face another human being in that way—exchanging eye expressions, quiet words, tenderness, comfort, joy—can be one of life's most rewarding experiences. Unlike the traditional clandestine affair, such dating is not a situational escalator leading inevitably to sexual intercourse, for there are many other behavioral options—a long walk, a trip to the museum, dinner together, and so on. For those for whom the appearance of marriage meets all their intimacy needs, dating after marriage presents difficulties. But we suggest that it be added to our options.

ENDURING INTIMACY: A relationship in which the intimate aspects evolve through years of trust and mutual respect. It may involve two or more persons of the same or opposite sex. The emphasis is on depth and loyalty with varying amounts of intensity and/or romance. The chances are that you can be truthful about almost everything, except when a part of your lifestyle definitely offends your enduring intimate.

EXTRAORBITAL INTIMACY: A close relationship with someone who is neither physically nor in fantasy a part of your daily life. The partner may be from out of town (old friend, new acquaintance met on a plane or a meeting, and so forth) or the intimacy may be superimposed at intervals on an established friendship (special togetherness meetings once or twice a year, though the relationship is much more casual the rest of the time). Extraorbital intimacies can be deeply honest, romantic, intense, comforting, reassuring, joyful, or any combination thereof. The concept allows two people to relate to one another free of the anxieties and problems that would almost inevitably result should the intimacy intrude on daily life.

HONESTY INTIMACY: A relationship in which those involved put truthfulness as their top priority. There will be total, near-absolute honesty even when the truth hurts. This means negating some social niceties and tends to exclude romance. It is an essential element in super-friendship, but may be temporary, whereas super-friendship also involves commitment.

LIBERATED MARRIAGE: As used in this book, a pair-bond in which each partner enjoys a private compartment with no strings attached, and is free to withhold information about private compartment activities. This is not so much a decision against honesty as it is a decision in favor of personal privacy and freedom. Liberated marriage is especially useful when, after several years, it is quite evident that there are significant differences between two partners in matters of need, desire, or conscience. Rather than sunder the bond, liberated marriage loosens the bond somewhat, with fewer expectations and more room for outside fulfillments.

MULTIPLE INTIMACIES: A lifestyle in which intimacies of various kinds coexist: enduring, temporary; romantic, honest; same sex, other sex; and so forth. A person may enjoy this lifestyle whether single or married. We believe that many persons are on the verge of realizing this potential, but fear that the concept involves disloyalty or some such less-than-honorable motivation. We affirm the positive aspects of multiple intimacies within a framework of integrity and responsibility.

MYTH OF THE SCARCITY OF LOVE: This is the popular belief that "love is scarce," which encourages hoarding. Hoarding, in turn, creates the very scarcity that was feared to begin with. The myth's premises are that each of us has a very limited amount of love to give, spend, or sell; that if this is divided among several people, each will get less; that love can be saved; and that in order to be valuable, true love must be exclusive. These premises are disputed in our chapter, "The Myth of the Scarcity of Love."

OPEN MARRIAGE: A pair-bond with maximum honesty and openness between partners. It stresses the need for both husband and wife to enjoy exciting involvements and activities outside the marriage. If there are extramarital adventures, these may be discussed with the spouse and in that sense are shared, but honesty is not exaggerated to the point of cruelty. The concept is discussed in the best-selling book, *Open Marriage,* by Nena and George O'Neill.

PAIR-BOND: A committed relationship with one other person. The most common example is marriage and the most common form is exclusive and possessive. In our view, pair-bonds do not need to exclude other intimate relationships in order to be fulfilling and valuable to the pair-bond partners.

PAIRING: An approach to other people with the goal of achieving transparency, openness, and closeness very quickly. See the book, *Pairing,* by George Bach and Ronald Deutsch.

ROMANTIC INTIMACY: A relationship between two persons in which the feeling of being in love comes first. Blunt honesty often defers to soft partial truths in the desire to please one's love partner and to enrich the romance.

SUPER-FRIEND: Someone with whom you have an enduring honesty-intimacy. This means that you relate with qualities like transparency, authenticity, and sharing of feelings. But, by our definition, it cannot be a primary pair-bond: that is, each person in a super-friendship must have a separate social life, separate friends, separate roots that nurture and thereby allow for the risks involved in the commitment to blunt honesty. It is primarily supportive and nonthreatening to other intimacies. Super-friends can be very much a part of one's life, or they can be extraorbital and enjoyed only sporadically.

UNDERGROUND: Going underground means that you believe that what you are doing is right, but you recognize that being open about it involves serious risks. We use the term in regard to extramarital intimacies and/or sex. The "occupation army" (conservative societal institutions) often has power over your job, your future opportunity to earn a living and to live in dignity; and, for millions, any public knowledge of their private lives would mean loss of custody of children, dissolution of their marriages, and so forth. But essential to the concept of underground is the lack of guilt and the support of peers who also accept the underground lifestyle as unsatisfactory but still the best available solution to a very difficult and complex problem.

WARM FUZZIES: From "A Fairytale" by Claude M. Steiner, included in this book. A Warm Fuzzy is something that makes you feel good and warm all over. In real life, Warm Fuzzies are primarily hugs and tender embraces, and also include tender and warm sex which brings a feeling of closeness and comfort. The nature of Warm Fuzzies is that they are self-regenerating. But if they aren't used, they tend to turn into Cold Pricklies. There are also such things as Imitation Warm Fuzzies. You can tell the difference when, having received one, you begin to feel cold and prickly all over.

ANALOGIES AND PARABLES

A Parable of Two Farms

Once upon a time, a young couple decided to live on a beautiful farm. The soil was rich and black and free of stones. From early May until mid-September, a summer sun warmed it except when the rains fell. And rain came neither too much nor too little.

The man and his wife were young and vigorous. They said, "With such soil and climate, two such healthy people will never need a thing beyond our farm, each other, and whatever children may happen to come."

They planted their seeds and worked hard. They had time for relaxation together. Good harvests came, with singing and thanksgiving.

The years passed, and the fertility of the once-rich soil diminished. Separately and unbeknownst to each other, the husband and wife cast envious glances toward the farm next door, which remained fertile with bumper crops of food. And as their cow produced less and less milk, they noticed how their neighbor's cow kept giving its daily plenty.

The farmer and his wife looked upon their dwindling yield and determined to work harder and harder. They carefully saved money to buy expensive fertilizer to revitalize the soil. Even so, each year's work was harder, and each year's yield was more meager than any before it.

The couple found their strength waning, and they said (more to themselves than to each other), "Why have our crops failed to respond to our hard work? Are we such bad farmers?" There was no answer.

They considered accepting the limitations of their farm, and supplementing their diet by buying food at the market, or bartering their hay for some delicacies. But the laws of the land said, "He who owns a farm must eat of the crops of that farm, and of no other farm." (Actually, this was a reform of the old law, which had demanded in addition that every bit of furniture must be built from the farm's timber, and mechanical appliances were not allowed.) The wife thought of her mother who could not have a washing machine, and she tried to feel lucky. The man thought of his father building the old homestead without modern tools, hewing each plank by hand from the stand of oak by the creek, and he tried to feel lucky. But in truth, both were sad. They could not escape the gnawing hunger: not hunger from lack of subsistence, but hunger for new and different foods. They wondered what made the soil so rich next door.

The man and his wife (more to themselves than to each other) thought: Shall we sever our relationship in order to leave the farm and

try elsewhere? (The law stated, "He whose land has grown insufficient must, in seeking new land, be exiled from his former land and his partner thereof and begin utterly anew.") They wished the law would be abolished, as the furniture law had been. It was a cruel law forcing hardworking farmers into a painful dilemma. For both the farmer and his wife had deep affection for this land, which they had cultivated, struggled with, and lived with these many years. Even though their land's yield no longer filled their needs, the land formed a special bond between them. Their children had waded in its winding creeks. Along its unique fencerows they had gathered hickory nuts each autumn. Each wind-whipped creak of the ancient farmhouse was warmly familiar, together with its leaks and drafts, and these, too, helped weave the comfortable fabric of home.

Meanwhile, the next-door couple continued to enjoy their sumptuous dinners and desserts, all home-grown.

But *our* couple, try as they might, could no longer coax beautiful food from their land. And each yearned for it.

"Why would it be bad to partake of food produced outside our farm?" the wife asked herself. "They have inspection now—the risk of parasites is small." And the more she thought of it, the more convinced she became that new food would put new life into her, and help her work more cheerfully on her farm.

As for her husband, he thought to himself, "I would like pork much better if I could have steak once in awhile." But food from outside was taboo and not a subject to be freely discussed. So they worked and they dreamed.

One day the farmer next door, well-fed and basically content, with pork as well as steak and strawberries and apples, saw a tempting picture in a gourmet magazine. "I'd love to taste some of them mangoes," he thought. "Pshaw," he sighed, "Anyone knows you can't raise tropical fruit on a New England farm!"

So the two couples farmed on, side by side, one relatively content but yearning for tropical fruit; the other living in quiet desperation with a monotonous diet of pork chops, potatoes, and memories.

Instant Manhood-Womanhood

Marriage, like the Marines, is felt by some young men to confer instant manhood. Becoming a parent is proof of virility, general sexual adequacy, normalcy, and adulthood. Or so it would seem.

For girls, marriage and pregnancy seem to say, "I'm a woman now—I can lead my own life." Or so it seems.

Alas, in our ritual-starved culture, marriage and parenthood are often the only puberty rites available. Rites of passage from childhood to adulthood have been meaningful experiences in various cultures both ancient and modern. But as a rite of passage, young marriage is a loser.

When people marry before or during the rather dramatic changes of late adolescence, they may marry one person and end up living with another one five years later—a significantly different personality in the same body, to which one is bound by the same legal contract, not to mention the diapers and the cat box.

Young people have been told that marriage is the only valid context for sex. Some of them really believe it. But marriage is not the only alternative.

Marriage is not necessary for sexual gratification.

Marriage is not necessary for significant, caring relationships which are passionate as well as idealistic.

Marriage is not an economic necessity.

Nor does it really prove one is a man or a woman or adequate or normal. It may, in many instances, merely prove that one is an idiot.

Marriage may be a good choice for two people whose personalities have stabilized, who know who they are and who the other is, whose priorities and commitments are clear, and who may want to rear children together.

But it doesn't prove a damned thing.

Celibacy, Adultery and Deviance

"Deviant" is differing from the norm or from the standards of society. Celibacy differs from the norm. Adultery differs from the standards of society. Adultery is socially deviant. Celibacy is statistically and biologically deviant. But let us not forget that excellence is also statistically and biologically deviant. And for our last example of deviance we offer this book.

Sex Is for . . .

Sex is for those in love. For those not in love sex is routinely condemned except in marriage. But how many marriage counselors insist that married people stop having sex as soon as love begins to fade; that you should refuse your eager partner as soon as you cannot honestly affirm you are in love? So I guess what we are really saying is that sex is for those who are either married or in love . . . and both is beautiful.

When Less Than 60 Percent Is Better Than Divorce

Denizens of our culture are programmed to hope that marriage will be a 100 percent affair. And our hopes determine our disappointments.

There can be no such thing as a 100 percent marriage. So stop being disappointed already, if that's why you're disappointed!

We do know some people who seem to have 90 percent. Their social and sexual desires and appetites are well-matched, year after year. And year after year, they share a wide range of mutual interests. Their lives are as close to oneness as can be. Yet each is a separate, real person! Of course, some of these marriages are symbiotic and mutual retreats from life—but that is not what we're describing here. In a successful 90 percent marriage, communication is honest and rewarding most of the time. This is the marriage described in popular magazines as the goal toward which all should presumably strive.

But many of us will, in fact, be happier if we can seek and accept less than 90 percent in marriage.

More of our marriages will be rewarding and worthwhile if we change the goals, relax the rules, and give more time outs.

Not only are most people not sexual athletes, they are not marriage athletes, either.

And if one can accept his or her marriage as a 50 or 60 percent relationship, that need not mean a 50 or 60 percent life! Far from it. That being the case, a 50 percent marriage may be well worth keeping.

After all, half of another person's time, energy, and emotion is a great deal. Even 25 percent is a lot, when you stop to think of it.

If It Works, It's Dangerous (If It's Dangerous, It Works)

Suicides are performed daily with common household drugs. An overdose of good medicine can kill. If it works, it's dangerous.

Love and sex are powerful stuff—and we all know that extramarital sex destroys marriages. At least, it's the peg on which the divorce and the neighborhood gossip are hung. We might have to look deeper for the real reasons: years of boredom, nagging, or viciousness.

But if it's dangerous, it also works! It is a well-documented fact that extramarital sex does enhance and save many marriages. Outside sex can be a source of passion and affirmation for those whose marriages are dull and routine, but still worth saving for other reasons. And even when the marriage is exciting, outside sex can help inside sex seem better, not necessarily because it is really better but just because it is different. As the transactional analysis people like to say, "You don't have to be sick to get better." You don't have to have a lousy marriage to also find other relationships rewarding.

The fact that people misuse their sexuality does not condemn it, just as the fact that people pop giant bottles of pills and are dead soon thereafter does not condemn the use of medication by responsible people.

Even though fire burns houses down, few of us choose to live in cold houses.

There are proper places for fires, of course, in fireplaces. But whereas traditional moralists would say yes, and the fireplace is monogamous marriage, we prefer another tack. To wit, the best fireplace is a strong, internal set of priorities. We would suggest, family first—but not necessarily last!

If monogamous marriage is the fireplace—as the traditionalists suggest—one may wind up with a fireplace without a fire. But if the fireplace is a strong set of personal priorities, it can contain whatever warmth one may find or create. A portable fireplace!

Cars Are Dangerous, Useful, and Fun

Cars kill millions, and maim even more. Some drivers use their autos as instruments of aggressive hostility. Out on the road, they can really show the world who takes the lead! They break the speed limits, pass going over hills, and run red lights. Everybody else—out of the way!

But most of us would be up in arms if a law were passed saying, "Because some people drive recklessly, no one may drive."

And we would feel irrationally limited if a law said, "You can drive your car to work—but not for fun. Vacations in the car are strictly prohibited!"

Our sexuality is also powerful, dangerous, useful, and fun.

This is true both of sex within marriage and of extramarital sex.

About sex within marriage, some moralists say, "Sex is for procreation only—never for recreation."

And about sex outside of marriage, they say, "Because many people have misused outside sex and wrecked marriages, no one may have outside sex."

Our definition of the responsible driver: even if his family is not in the car, he knows how important he is to them and takes care to return home safe and sound.

Our definition of the responsible extramarital lover would be much the same.

Whether in driving or in sex, risks can never be wholly eliminated from life. So shall we stop driving?

What Makes Sex Legitimate?

Some say that only marriage makes sex legitimate. Extremists believe that sex is inherently evil but is glorified by the institution of marriage—somewhat the way that killing is inherently evil but is glorified by the state of war.

Most of us, however, have a far more complex attitude toward human sexual behavior, although our Puritan tradition dictates that we start with the concept that it is, indeed, inherently dirty and can be made clean by meeting certain requirements. The variation among authorities as to what requirements make sex legitimate is myriad:

married only must have same religion sex okay with spouse even if not in love same sex okay if in love must be either in love or married hand caressing okay but no oral sex masturbation okay if not married penis/vagina only vibrators okay if single same sex okay if no heterosexual partner available oral sex okay for homosexuals vibrators okay if married casual sex is okay if homosexual oral sex okay if married must come from same socio-economic status no dildos extramarital sex okay if spouse is unavailable for six months or more must use contraception dildos okay if impotent casual sex okay if neither has a primary relationship anal sex okay if married must not use contraception casual sex is okay if heterosexual dogs okay if no other sex partner available group sex okay if same race and couples only anal sex okay for homosexuals different races okay if one-to-one and meaningful relationship no animals

We have a different approach. We believe that any and all sexual expressions are legitimate providing that the sexual activity does not infringe on the rights of others. We see no reason to continue our association of morality with the particular way in which persons express themselves sexually. This gives harmless physical acts an inordinate amount of ethical power. Morality has more to do with things like love, responsibility, and sensitivity to the needs of others. How do you feel? What do you think makes sex legitimate?

Whose Court? Yours? Mine? or Ours Only?

In an affair, the intimacy can for some people ideally be just that: no mortgage, no movers, no helping with homework, no financial squabbles. That doesn't make it automatically bad, anymore than playing tennis is bad. In order to have the right to play tennis should you also have to endure the hassle of building and maintaining your own court? Or should you have to make a lifelong commitment to play with only one partner? Should you have to take tennis seriously? With contraception and precautions against contracting venereal disease, sex for some people is sometimes serious, but other times just plain fun, like a casual game of tennis. The point, in terms of transiency, is that people are frequently away from their home court, even if they have one. And when they're in their home court, since they have just one helper to tighten the net, repair the cracks, hose it down, trim the grass around the edges, repaint the lines, and contribute to the time payments—they would prefer playing with a different partner for a change at a different court that doesn't remind them of all that responsibility. Others, of course, enjoy the pride of their home-built court and prefer playing with only one partner. Why must they be labeled good or bad? Different strokes for different folks.

Distancing and Divorce

For many couples divorce is the best solution. For them, divorce is a courageous decision and not a sign of weakness. For many, divorce has meant a beautiful new beginning free of crushing anxieties and hostilities. We all know that divorce can also cause misery for some individuals. We are neither for nor against divorce. We merely want to present another option for the millions who find themselves trapped in their lives going through the motions of intimacy and togetherness without meaning. They are able to enjoy neither the fruits of freedom nor the joys of intimacy. To them, presenting an acceptable image becomes a thankless lifetime task.

To some persons caught in such a bind, distancing, either temporary or as a lifestyle, may present an attractive option. (a) Limited distancing when space and money are very restricted. Such distancing may be accomplished just by agreement that you need separateness to think and contemplate the best outcome of a faltering relationship. Each might treat the other as a respected member of a cooperative, discussing tasks and exchanging pleasantries, as acquaintances would, without pretending intimacy. Eating may or may not be arranged at different times; or sometimes together and sometimes separate. Each would be responsible for certain specifics, and not be responsible to the other for time not needed to live up to the new contract. After the interval is over, responses are elicited and the next step taken, whatever seems best for the particular couple. (b) Distancing with more access to space and money. This may mean having separate rooms or even a separate apartment for one spouse. One counselor wrote about advising a couple to get divorced and to jointly rent a far inferior apartment to which either of them could retreat when they became annoyed with each other. For these people this odd type of divorce had a joyous outcome. Since they were officially divorced, whenever they saw each other it was by choice and even more exciting. Of course, for other couples this would not work at all. (c) Distancing with Compartment Four. This can be used as a way of distancing as well as a way of maintaining closeness. For distancing, Compartment Four can be used for major emotional gratifications, ones that may equal or surpass the gratifications of marriage, but in no way be a substitute for marriage. Compartment Four can also be a very tiny part of one's life, but an important one because it allows for that privacy, or potential privacy, to exist within the contract, thereby avoiding both guilt and contamination of a basically honest, beautiful, and intimate relationship.

Of course there will always be those who don't want distancing, don't even want a small compartment of privacy. For them the all-or-nothing law reigns supreme. The reality is, however, that few of the millions who aim for total intimacy are able to enjoy that phenomenon decade after decade. Not every person is capable of a sustained, truly intimate relationship. And millions more might be capable with someone else, but definitely not with the one to whom they are currently married. Many make the decision to seek out the person. And some find the person. But for everyone who does, there are hundreds who never find the needle in the haystack.

We believe that many persons would be happier partly married; in fact, this was specifically stated by many persons whom we interviewed. These people indicated in a joking manner that they really wanted to be just partly married. Actually, when questioned further, they indicated that indeed they would like to take the concept seriously, but were hesitant to use that term. They said quite frankly that they wanted "to have their cake and eat it." We affirm that that should be a valid option for every couple, provided, of course, that both partners agree to the contract.

The essence of the distancing message is that it may offer authenticity to a temporary or a permanent reality; it may offer a potential for fulfillment; it may break through an extremely hypocritical and stifling marriage relationship.

Too many persons we interviewed were paying an exorbitant price for the image of intimacy. Going places (and staying home) together without enjoying each other's company. Denying oneself any intimate relationships at all, since marriage intimacy is an exclusive one. Distancing offers a chance to redefine, either for awhile or for a lifetime, a particular marriage relationship, with the needs of each partner given serious consideration. Being partly married may be a good option for some, but we recognize that many others will be adamant about the all-or-none law. We urge that marriage become flexible to meet the various needs of humans rather than trying to make all humans fit into a simple traditional concept of marriage.

Free Time

John, Jim, Jill, and Jane all had some free time.

John went to the bar and had some drinks with the boys.
Jim went to the track to bet on the horses.
Jill went to the dark room to develop pictures.

Jane went to a motel and made love.

John runs the risk of becoming an alcoholic.
Jim runs the risk of becoming a compulsive gambler.
Jill runs the risk of allowing photography to interfere with her other
    obligations.
Jane runs the risk of allowing her love-making to interfere with her
    other obligations.

John may come home happy, sad, or indifferent.
Jim may come home happy, sad, or indifferent.
Jill may come home happy, sad, or indifferent.
Jane may come home happy, sad, or indifferent.

But even if John, Jim, and Jill consistently came home late and
irritable and even if Jane consistently came home on time, radiant and
loving—Jane is the only one who will consistently be condemned in the
mass media and advice columns. Directly or indirectly it will be clear
that Jane is bad and something very bad will happen to her or her loved
ones. To show the beneficial effects of extramarital sex is strictly taboo.

Mystery Novels and Sex

When you read a good mystery novel, you may enjoy every page
and still not want to read the same novel again and again. You may
prefer a new mystery with a new murder and a new solution to the crime.

Some people are curious about how a person will be in bed, somewhat like being curious about whodunit. It may be lots of fun finding
out how someone is in bed, even if after the curiosity is satisfied, there
may be no desire to return to bed a second or third time.

Sometimes you are very disappointed in bed with someone. It may
be just okay, not great at all, or even a bummer. Sometimes you get
hooked into a lousy mystery novel, and wish you hadn't wasted the time
reading it.

Although many people, influenced by our traditional romantic concepts of sex, are indeed turned off by the comparison of a mystery novel
and sex, there are others who can and do enjoy casual sexual encounters.

And when an encounter is unfulfilling, it may be chalked up as "Well, you can't win them all!" rather than feeling that one had done a bad or wrong thing. Casual sex involves a certain risk. If some people are willing to take the risk, why should other people be so concerned?

We give lip service to the thought that intimacy between two persons is far more dependent on the shared thoughts and feelings than shared genitals. Yet, when put to the test, when genitals are shared without intimacy, then the genital sharing is put down because there was no intimacy! When two persons are intimate, sharing thoughts and feelings, then adding sex adds a unique dimension. But sex need not be limited to special intimate relationships, and enjoying casual sex need not destroy one's capacity for intimate sex.

Many who are avid readers of mystery novels also enjoy Shakespeare and Goethe. One more case of the "both/and" option replacing the "either/or" alternative.

Sex and Hooks

We have, as advocates of freer marriage, been repeatedly accused of treating sex as a physical act only and neglecting the emotional hooks that complicate all human relationships. But we do acknowledge the hooks in most sexual encounters. Such hooks are also inherent in money and power transactions. People become deeply emotional about sex but also about money and power. Many a husband has loused up his sex life in the pursuit of money or power or both. But that does not prevent people from discussing money without always mentioning the hooks. Not everyone gets hooked on money, power, or sex. Some persons can deal with any of the three without getting hooked.

Although the literature would probably put sex first, it has been our experience that more people can learn to control sex than money or power. But, whatever, all three risk deep destructive hooks. Does the husband of an ambitious political aspirant have more chance of a good sex life at home than the husband of a woman who has an occasional casual affair when out of town? Does the wife of an ambitious salesman determined to outdo all competitors have a better chance for a happy sex life than the wife of a nine to five worker who has a sex partner 600 miles away whom he sees three times a year?

Adultery & Other Private Matters
200

Sex may or may not be emotionally complicated. Persons may or may not be able to deal with sex using clear contracts and integration into a responsible lifestyle. The same is true with money and power. Some can resist the temptation to go forever onward and upward without recognizing the hurts along the way. Some are able to control ambition and only seek money or power to the point of enhancing love relationships and never to the point of destroying relationships. Others get hooked and seek money, power, and sex to the point of destroying those whom they love. We acknowledge hooks. We affirm they can be avoided by some people, and with understanding, by many more.

Reveats and Revsexts

Some people take sex seriously all the time. They regard sex with great reverence, and may be called Revsexts. They may be likened to the Reveats who regard eating with great reverence. They eat only two meals a day. Before each meal they have a reverent ceremony. There is no eating between meals. There are no casual meals. There are no snacks! One should be grateful for each morsel of food and never under any circumstances treat eating lightly. Never eat for fun. To eat a hot dog at the ball game is immoral beyond belief. They simply cannot understand how some people can take eating so casually. They are convinced that someday, somehow, their digestive systems will rebel and they will be sorry for their sinful deeds. They observe all the fat people and the people with ulcers, and they are convinced they are right. Of course they too have some fat persons and some ulcer patients—but at least they do all they can to eat properly and with reverence.

The Revsexts use the same techniques. They point out the unhappy people who take sex casually and try to prove a correlation. They do not talk about the happy people who enjoy sex for fun. Like the Reveats, they admit that some who take sex very seriously are also unhappy and also have sexual problems, but at least they do all they can to have sex properly and with reverence.

Sexual Monogamy and the One-child Family

As a parent, you can love your quiet, artistic child and his sister who is exuberant, loud, and athletic. No one says to you, "How can you really love him when you say you love her? It's not possible to love two children at the same time!"

Why should the same capacity that makes us good parents suddenly make us naughty people when we express love for more than one adult?

After all, most of the arguments for sexual monogamy could also be used to argue for one-child families:

1. It isn't fair to take love away from the spouse.
   (It isn't fair to have a second child—this takes love away from your only child.)

2. Outside sex is a flight from real intimacy with one's spouse.
   (Having or adopting additional children is an avoidance of giving complete attention and intimacy to the child you already have.)

3. Outside sex can lead to jealousy and weaken the marriage relationship.
   (The only child may be jealous of any additional children in the home. That's awful!)

4. Money spent on lovers—for presents, evenings out, hotel rooms, and other things—siphons needed resources away from the home.
   (Money spent on additional children will deprive your only child of things he wants and needs.)

5. Outside sex or romance creates internal conflicts of interest that most people can't handle.
   (Bringing more children into the home creates conflicts of interest in the parents' minds—and most parents won't be able to handle this conflict. What if you have two sick or unhappy children at once? How can you ever handle it?)

6. It isn't the cheap physical stuff that makes affairs dangerous—it's the possibility of emotional involvement.
   (If you have more than one child, it's all right to hug and kiss them all—but be sure to reserve your emotional involvement for only one.)

7. It isn't romance and friendship that makes affairs dangerous—

it's the sexual involvement. Physical intimacy must be reserved for only one person.

(It's fine to be friends with all your kids, just so long as only one of them gets hugs and kisses.)

And so on. Are you convinced that having more than one child is immoral? Or dangerous? Or will tear you apart emotionally? Even those who advocate one or two child families—like Zero Population Growth—are in favor of adoption. There are many people in the world in need of love—and not all of them are children.

INDEX

Warm Fuzzies, 54–58
Warner, Silas L., 131
*Who's Afraid of Virginia
Wolff?*, 20
Women
    sexuality of, 152

single, 22–33, 43, 90
status of, 8, 9, 42, 62–63

Your Fear of Love, 13, 133